"The power of this beautifully written book lingers long after its last page has been read. It is a love story in the best sense of that phrase. In his telling the story of Will and Hannah Greaves, Dr. Tyrrell gives us a tool for examining the experience of intimacy in our own lives—its seasons, its early illusions and later passions, its power to heal and transform. I recommend this book enthusiastically."

Sean D. Sammon, F.M.S.
Vicar General, Marist Brothers

"This is one of those rare and thoughtful books that reaches deep into an understanding of intimacy as experienced day to day in human life with its harshness and its joys. Through a biographical perspective of two individuals faithful to ordinary life, Dr. Tyrrell explores intimacy, the 'experience of being with others,' as essential in the formation of each person as individual and in relationship.

"This is a serious book to be read meditatively for its wealth of insight and wisdom about the human journey."

Katie Kelley, Ph.D.
Grace Institute

"I congratulate Thomas Tyrrell for addressing the formative implications of intimacy. Students and practitioners alike will find in these pages, as the title of my own book indicates, 'formation of the heart.' I recommend reading the text. It conveys not only solid information about intimacy but wisdom for living."

Professor Adrian van Kaam, Ph.D.
Founder of the Science of Formation
Professor, Duquesne University

"In Will and Hannah's 'adventure of intimacy,' Tyrrell concludes that our only requirement in life is to simply learn to be ourselves with all our gifts and limits. This is acted out in relationship with another. Such a relationship will bring intimacy, but the cost is suffering. In the story of Will and Hannah, Tyrrell has discovered many golden nuggets of wisdom and given them to us."

John A. Rich., M.M.
Spiritual Director, Author

"Once again, Thomas Tyrrell serves the community of faith well, nourishing us with the substantial insights of his own study and pastoral practice. *The Adventure of Intimacy* is a rich resource for soul-work professionals—pastoral ministers, spiritual directors, therapists, formation personnel—that can also be shared directly with those in their care. Lay persons, vowed religious, and priests will find their experience reflected and illumined in the life examples Tyrrell draws on."

Evelyn Eaton Whitehead. Ph.D.
James D. Whitehead. Ph.D.
Co-authors, *Community of Faith*

"Intimacy is hard work and Hannah and Will's lives attest to the fact that it is a lifetime endeavor. By allowing each other to 'be,' they transformed themselves from separateness to oneness without losing either experience. Tyrrell places the good wine of intimacy before us to taste and see. The wine promises to be both fragrant and hearty, to nourish and sustain us."

Peg Renner
Ph.D. Candidate, Theologian, Therapist

"In an age that seems to be dominated by the spectacular, Thomas J. Tyrrell's *The Adventure of Intimacy* calls us to see again the ordinary, the everydayness of intimacy. The story of Hannah and Will's relationship offers us wisdom for the everydayness of our lives. Their school of daily experiences eclipses pop psychology and self-help books."

Vincent Bilotta, Ph.D.
President of Formation Consultation Services, Inc.

"This book realistically addresses the difference between infatuation and mature intimacy. As I have found from experience, the latter is inseparable from the cross in one form or another. I felt particularly impressed by the author's recognition that the classical writings of St. John of the Cross have much to say to our search for lasting and meaningful relationships."

Susan Muto, Ph.D.
Author, Executive Director, The Epiphany Association

Thomas J. Tyrrell

THE ADVENTURE OF INTIMACY

A Journey through Broken Circles

XXIII
TWENTY-THIRD PUBLICATIONS
Mystic, Connecticut 06355

Twenty-Third Publications
185 Willow Street
P.O. Box 180
Mystic, CT 06355
(203) 536-2611
800-321-0411

ISBN 0-89622-532-1
Library of Congress Catalog Card Number 92-60891
Printed in the U.S.A.

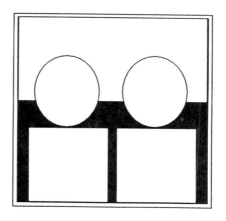

Preface

The Adventure of Intimacy: A Journey Through Broken Circles,
which is concerned with spirituality in the context of relationship, arose from the feedback I received concerning another volume I wrote some years ago, *Urgent Longings.* That
book focuses on the experience of infatuation and its role in
the formation of intimacy with self, other, and God. Based on
lectures I gave to Roman Catholic clergy and religious, it is a
study of the phenomenon of reciprocal infatuation and its relationship to mature intimacy and to one's presence to self,
other, and God in the context of religious life. The project
was oriented toward helping religious professionals in their
struggles to relate to one another and to the Holy.

The response to *Urgent Longings* has revealed the myopia of my vision. I received letters and phone calls from Roman Catholic religious professionals who had experienced infatuation and had discovered a deeper capacity to be intimate in both their prayer and relational lives. I also received the same message from married and single laypeople representing a variety of professions, occupations, and faith-perspectives. In the decade since the original study was published, people have communicated the joy, pain, and struggle encountered in their search to find a loving response from each other and God. They taught me that although there are clear and distinct vocational differences between secular and religious forms of life, the struggle to realize meaningful, integrated, and intimate relationships is in large measure vocationally blind. Dynamically, celibate and non-celibate individuals face the same struggle in that search for intimacy, which is also a search for meaning, depth, and personal integrity.

The lessons I have learned during this past decade are presented in this new book, *The Adventure of Intimacy*. Simultaneously, a wholly revised edition of *Urgent Longings* has been published.

In preparing *The Adventure of Intimacy*, considerable use has been made of experiential data. Specifically, people of various ages, both religious professionals and laity, have graciously contributed their experiences of relational intimacy in a variety of situations. The thematic structure that emerged from these data is interwoven with anecdotal data from the lives of two people who served as models of psychological and spiritual integration for much of my adult life: Hannah Bently Browning and John William ("Will") Greaves, my maternal grandparents.

I recognize that this approach carries with it possibilities of misunderstanding. One is that this present study will be looked upon as a biography; it is not intended as such.

Rather, it is my hope that the simplicity of Hannah and Will's story and the depth of their relationship will serve notice to anyone who is tempted to abandon the call to love in favor of "achievement." Accomplishment, authority, personal power and control, the accumulation of possessions, indeed all of the activities and values of competitive life have their place. But in the arena of everyday relating, where the depth of intimacy is formed and found, the pursuit of "achievement" can become a formidable obstacle. Married or "monk," relating to self, other, or God with a competitive (ego) attitude will destroy the seed of intimacy found in the simple acts of daily relating. The story of Hannah and Will's journey gives ample testimony to this truth.

Another possible misunderstanding in my approach is that this book might be viewed as a primer on the spirituality of marriage. Here I can only advise the reader that if either Hannah or Will were alive, each would be gracious and appreciative, but would consider the model-maker a bit "daft" for proposing them as models. If, for example, you were at a public gathering and selected either of them for praise, each would regard it as unwarranted and unwelcomed intrusion. Hannah would probably be publicly respectful, then privately pray for your recovery if she and "the old man" were regarded in this way. Will would most likely invite you for a walk or a cup of tea (unless you were a bit too persistent, in which case he would suggest a few glasses of beer) and then gently but firmly recommend that other models or sources of inspiration be located—quickly! Hannah and Will were simple, hard-working, fun-loving, and humble people who would not present themselves as an example of anything that might exalt them above others. They were not saints, but their faith deeply enriched their relational life; and they lived that life in an ordinary, simple, and humble way.

Essentially, I am telling their story because it lends substance to the data I have collected on the experience of relational intimacy. Their story is worth telling because it is a story of our universal struggle for a loving response. It is a story of intimacy, a story of the pain and sorrow that occur when our competitive ego intrudes itself upon those to whom we are trying to relate.

Further, I anticipate that through their story you will begin to draw upon your own experiences. I hope you will be touched by their life together as it unfolds in the following pages and begin to see in them the wonder of life that is at the heart of intimacy. More important, I hope their story will awaken in you the story of other ordinary, gentle, good people with whom you are now acquainted. If it does, I would ask you to venture a few pointed questions about their relational life. In particular, ask them about their struggle to be intimate with the people they care for. I expect that in looking to those who are our original formation team in life we learn much of what is required for relating to others. In a mobile culture such as ours we do not often have access to this team. So, to those who belong to an extended-family-stretched-too-far, I share Hannah and Will's story in the hope of facilitating your own process of discovery.

The basic experience addressed within these pages is relational intimacy. The perspective from which I write continues to be psychological, specifically, the descriptive, experiential approach. However, the interpretation of psychological content is offered from within a different scientific perspective. I am referring to the science of Formative Spirituality, although I intend to focus only on spirituality within the context of relationship.

The present book is intended to make clearer, through Hannah and Will's story, the natural formation forces that affect the development of our relational life, but it is not intended to be a document on human development. The revised edition of *Urgent Longings* serves that function, presenting a more systematic study of the formation forces that are at work in our lives. The purpose of *The Adventure of Intimacy* is that you might be assisted in your struggle with the experience of intimacy.

The struggle changes as the developmental phases of our lives unfold. At the beginning of our journey we wrestle with the experience of infatuation; the data collected for that experience is presented in *Urgent Longings*. The material addressing infatuation is referred to throughout *The Adventure of Intimacy*, particularly in Chapter 5 which focuses on the ascetics of intimacy. However, the data collected on the experience of intimacy suggests that as we search for relationships of meaning, depth, and integrity in the unfolding of our lives we experience certain moments which, over time, form our understanding of intimacy: a sense of being with and for others where we discard the mask of our public or personal identities, revealing ourselves as vulnerable. It is an experience where we are present to others in such a way that we feel understood, known, accepted; where we experience the emotional or physical warmth of nearness and the freedom to be separate. Intimacy involves disclosure with its attendant words and gestures, but also occurs during moments of silence, where a mutual sense of communication occurs. Such experiential moments seem to form the basis for our hunger for intimacy and are in sharp contrast to the eroticized images portrayed in the popular media.

I believe these experiential themes also reflect your story of intimacy. And I am confident that much of what is presented about Hannah and Will's life will resonate with your experience and those who are your guides and models on the relational journey. This book is written in the hope that it will assist you as you travel across the horizon of relationship; for the relational journey can be a deeply spiritual experience.

This book is also written for those who are charged with the awesome and difficult task of providing a professional service such as spiritual direction, psychological or pastoral counseling. To these professional groups I feel an obligation to mention that there are many implicit assumptions within these pages. The chapter titles and themes provide a clue to my fundamental assumption that the realization of intimacy is a struggle that requires a willingness to wrestle with our wounded nature. I also confess to being inspired by an existential approach that presumes that the desire to be intimate also involves a willingness to suffer. I am not speaking exclusively of the psychological approach to experiences such as loneliness, rejection, aloneness, anger, etc., but of a different approach, one that enables forms of suffering such as these to be seen in the light of their inherently creative potential. These pages presume and to some extent address a phenomenon that must be called *creative suffering*. An exclusively psychological understanding of relational intimacy and suffering is inadequate.

With this in mind, you will see that the point of departure that I am taking with this book and with its companion text, *Urgent Longings,* cannot be based exclusively on a psychological approach, but requires another interpretive schema to comprehend the experience of intimacy in all of its richness and depth.

If this book is for spiritual directors and counselors, pastoral as well as psychological, it is primarily directed to the laity and religious professionals who are themselves trying to live relational lives of depth and meaning. You will notice the themes contained within the chapters: dreams, journey, choice, illusion, darkness, struggle, brokenness, love, anger, complaisance, pride (to name only some). If you have wrestled with these experiences in your struggle to be intimate, I anticipate this book will be of assistance, for it is clear that in your search for intimacy you are not living at the surface of your relational life.

Hannah and Will's is a story not so much of two particular people as it is of the "oneness" between them. On this point, if you are a religious professional, I risk chastisement. I am aware that very many religious professionals are working hard to relate to others and not get trapped in a compromise of vows. It would be a mistake to think that married people are "ahead of the game" simply because they have a permanent life companion. In fact, in the world of relationship the married *and* celibate life have many difficulties in common, particularly a common call to simplicity and relational depth: *to love our neighbor as our self* in the ethic of that call.

To both the married and celibate person I offer a reminder that the final end of the spiritual journey is neither companionship nor individuality, but oneness. Here, I unabashedly borrow from George MacDonald's *Unspoken Sermons,* where he states: ". . . there can be no unity, no delight of love, no harmony, no good in being, where there is but one. *Two* at least are needed for oneness."[1] When I have had the audacity to state this publicly, many have offered this correction: MacDonald meant the "individual" and the "divine," not necessarily two "individual" people. I will not argue the point, but simply offer an encouraging nod to those people of integrity—laity, religious, and clergy—who are struggling hard to live healthy and holy relational lives.

The command of Jesus to enter deeply into the richness that is found in relationship offers a challenge to the celibate and the non-celibate person; it also offers much that is common to both. One need not sacrifice individuality or get lost in relationship in order to be intimate; this, I think, is the testament and challenge of Hannah and Will's story.

Dedication

"This made it more likely that [it had been] a true vision; for instead of making common things look commonplace, as a false vision would have done, it had made common things disclose the wonderful that was in them."

George MacDonald
The Shadows

With this quotation in mind I dedicate this book to
Karen, Donna, Jennifer, Brian, and Kevin

Through the following pages I have drawn upon the life of two people about whom you have some familiarity but little direct experience: Hannah Bently Browning and John William Greaves, your great-grandparents. Perhaps in learning about Hannah and Will you will see the "wonderful" in them that I see in each of you.

This book is also dedicated to the memory of Rose Rootes and her son Joseph Rootes who died while this text was in preparation.

Acknowledgments

I would like to express my appreciation to those whose encouragement, support, and assistance have made this project possible:

To Carol, my best friend, wife, and most challenging and supportive critic: sincere thanks for your help and patience.

To Louis Horvath, Mary B. Walsh, Sr. Joan Dreisbach, O.S.F., Ronald Karney, Ph.D., the staff and patients of the Villa St. John Vianney Hospital, as well as former staff and residents of the House of Affirmation who shared their experiences and listened to my lectures: you helped to clarify and enrich my thinking and your support kept the project moving.

To the members of the spiritual study group to which Carol and I belonged: Sr. Dolores Beatty, G.N.S.H., Theresa Helldorfer, D. Min. (cand.), Martin Helldorfer, D. Min., Sr. Joan Koliss, O.S.F., and Rev. Charles O'Hara, M.A.: your understanding of the spiritual life has been challenging, enriching, and corrective.

To James Murdock and Dennis Devlin for their financial research, John van Bemmel and Joanne Cornell for their editing, and Connie Enoches for her corrections.

A special note of appreciation is offered to Diane Rootes whose typing skills turned my scribbling into something intelligible. I would also like to thank her for the gift of her caring and challenging presence in our family.

Finally, to Bill Greaves, Elsie Dunham, Hilda Tyrrell, Rose Rootes, Thomas Greaves, James Greaves, and Joan Connelly, the children of Hannah and Will: a very special note of thanks is offered. Each of you worked your memories and dug through albums, dresser drawers, and the attic to help in the reconstruction of Hannah and Will's story. While the "Joseph's Coat" I have stitched is essentially my design and not intended to be comprehensive, I hope it is reasonably true to your memory and experience. My gratitude, however, is not confined to your being historical resources. Each of you has formed a significant part of my own formation story. I am very grateful for the gift of your presence in my life and I pray I am able to reflect the values that each of you labored so hard to impart during my early formation.

Contents

Preface   *v*

Introduction   1

Chapter 1
The Adventure of Intimacy   12

Chapter 2
A Journey Across the Horizon of Relationship   29

Chapter 3
Obedience to an Interior Vocation   42

Chapter 4
A Passion for Reform   58

Chapter 5
The Ascetics of Intimacy   70

Chapter 6
Intimate Circles   90

Notes   111

Selected Bibliography   118

To reach satisfaction in all
desire its possession in nothing
To come to the knowledge of all
desire the knowledge of nothing
To come to possess all
desire the possession of nothing
To arrive at being all
desire to be nothing

—The Ascent of Mount Carmel

Introduction

These words were written more than four centuries ago by St. John of the Cross, a 16th-century contemplative monk whose stated purpose was to educate and guide people of faith who had embarked on the spiritual journey.[1] His instructions continue to have relevance to those who seek relationships of simplicity, integrity, meaning, and depth.

When I first heard the teachings of John of the Cross, they seemed harsh and irrelevant for contemporary life. Ascetic concepts such as "mortification" and "dispossession" belong

1

to a bygone era, I thought. The spiritual experience of "dark nights" speak to an archaic Roman Catholic romanticism, or perhaps to a select few who are able to live the monastic life. "Contemplation" seemed an experience that happened only to those who could endure the harsh medieval discipline through which it was taught. I never considered that his wisdom might have direct application to the daily unfolding of our capacity to be intimate.

Sometime between the mid-1970s and the early 1980s, my appreciation for the teaching of John of the Cross began to develop. This shift took place primarily because of the perceptive intervention of our study group, which had embarked on a study of his major works with the intention of discerning his relevance to contemporary life.[2]

Beyond the thoughtful reflection of the study group, I am cautious about identifying any other personal events that also may have nurtured my appreciation for the relevance of John of the Cross to life today. To cite specific personal experience would arrogate an authority and inspiration I do not think exist. But I have a story to tell about a series of events and family recollections that made me better able to appreciate what this gifted and perceptive saint can teach us.

The first event occurred during a family reunion in the early 1980s. I had not been back to visit my mother's relatives since my grandmother's funeral in 1976. For as long as I can remember, my grandparents, Hannah and Will Greaves, had occupied a homey little frame house at 54 George St., Green Island, New York. Their house was torn down in the late 1970s after they both had died. The house was razed to clear the way for a bridge connecting Troy to Latham, New York. Where my grandfather Will had once planted tomatoes, children now played basketball, protected from the rain by the bridge, high over their heads, that now spans the Hudson River.

With the exception of the bridge, the village of Green

Island had not changed much since the 1930s. The Sweet Shop had had a facelift and a name change. Picarello's grocery store looked as I remembered it, although it too had undergone the transition to new ownership. Here and there were signs of change, but by and large "the Village" had the comforting sameness that helps preserve childhood memories. The lone exception to my recollection of the past was a wide ribbon of concrete and steel that now formed a canopy above the spot formerly occupied by my grandparents' home. Where so many warm, wonderful, and painful events had once occurred, now stood a concrete abutment, a small playground, and a chain-link fence.

I had known of the project to build the bridge and was grateful that neither Hannah or Will had lived to see it. I do not know how long I gazed in disbelief, but was jolted out of my reverie by my aunt Joan's comment. "It's all gone," she intoned with a sense of resignation. "It's all gone. I was unable to drive past this spot for the longest time," she continued. "I just couldn't stop remembering." Now, here we were, in front of what was once 54 George St., and we were both remembering.

Hannah and Will's youngest children, Joan and Jim, twins and six years my senior, were born in the old frame house, so this pilgrimage was for Joan more meaningful and, I think, more painful than it was for me. "It's all gone, except the memories," she offered.

"Yeah," I added, "I remember when we almost burned the place down trying to toast marshmallows."

"You would remember that!

"I was so scared Dad would find out," she continued. Actually, it was probably no more than dropping a match after holding it a bit too long trying to coax the last bit of flame into creating that delicious brown crust we both loved as children. I had not given much thought to the old back kitchen for decades. Now, here we were exchanging childhood memories in a bittersweet reverie about the wonderful events that touched us both.

I do not know how long Joan and I stared at the spot once occupied by the old house. But I recall feeling the same way later that day when Joan took a memento out of her closet, the address plate that hung above the entrance to Hannah and Will's: 54. Joan went on to recall that each of Hannah and Will's seven children had managed to retrieve some small souvenir of their life there. The state of New York had paid the surviving relatives for this disruption to their histories; that, plus a small savings account meant that Hannah and Will's estate amounted to $2300 or so bequeathed to each of their seven surviving children.

That evening as Hannah and Will's family gathered, the reminiscing continued; each son or daughter added a different event or a slightly different perspective on one or other occurrence. As the evening wore on, many stories were exchanged, some intended to bring the other siblings up to date, others picking up on the threads of remembrance Joan and I had begun to weave earlier that day at the house site. What emerged that evening was not just the retelling of a series of happy or sad memories, but a family portrait. Hannah and Will's children were telling their individual stories. But each was also relating a formation story of two very different people who, individually and out of the intimacy of their relationship, had touched the lives of each one in that room in a very special way. That evening I once again became aware that the legacy of Hannah and Will went far beyond any sum of money or material possession.

Hannah and Will owned very little, yet they had given something special to each member of their family, something that continued to live long after they had died. They each had very little formal education—three years between them—yet they had passed on a library of wisdom that continued to affect the personal journey of their children and grandchildren. They had not achieved fame or wealth, and in the world beyond 54 George Street they had really not amounted to much. But the love and respect they earned from their family and friends were a clear testimonial to the intimacy, integrity, and awareness they had developed in their journey through life.

Since the reunion, there have been a host of conversations with the friends and relatives of Hannah and Will. I regret that I have not committed each reminiscence to tape or paper. But the events I did retain have served to validate that as their lives unfolded, from courtship to funeral, a series of ordinary events occurred, joyous and painful, that formed in each an ever-deepening sense of faith. I do not know if either one had ever undergone a dark-night experience. But it has become strikingly clear to me that in traveling across the horizon of human existence each had grown in detachment from the *striving* for achievement and possession that infects so many of us today. And in the process, the struggle we call life, both Hannah and Will grew in simplicity, integrity, and in their ability to love others.

What follows is a series of reflections on the intimacy that evolved in Hannah and Will's relationship. Yet, as I stated earlier, this volume is not intended to be biographical. Rather, I offer a reflection on the unfolding experience of intimacy, of which Hannah and Will's 65-year journey is an example. It is not a comprehensive personal story, for there are too many details of their lives I simply do not know. But their lives, as revealed to me through their children, in-laws, and friends, have helped me to develop a deeper grasp of the experience of intimacy and of its significance for our spiritual growth and development. Their lives may provide instruction in the teaching of John of the Cross for those who are seeking relationships of meaning, integrity, simplicity, and depth. I hope their story will prompt you to ask questions of your own parents and grandparents not on how to accumulate possessions, but in how to *be* with others. I am hopeful that people who are struggling with the experience of intimacy might look once more to the guidance of John of the Cross and find the practical wisdom needed to cope with our achievement- and possession-oriented culture.

There are six reflections intended to speak to the experience of intimacy as it unfolds in the course of life. The first, "The Adventure of Intimacy," addresses the posturing and false expectations we encounter when we are inspired by an infatuated dream, as opposed to a more selfless and caring vision of reality. The story of how these expectations are resolved is also the story of how we confront each other's pride. The chapter also describes how we exercise the choice to confront and facilitate the emergence of authenticity and freedom in our intimate relationships. In this chapter we examine a certain kind of suffering, one that must be endured if our "false selves" are to be dispossessed and the selves of authenticity and freedom are to find expression.

Chapter 2, "A Journey Across the Horizon of Relationship," continues the examination of the suffering we encounter in our relational life. The phenomenon of *complaisance* is introduced. Simply put, complaisance is the narcissistic action of the competitive self in its need to avoid pain and resist change. Our natural inclination to distort reality, develop false identities, and create illusions of permanence is presented as a function of complaisance. It is examined as the work of the dynamic inspired by the self of pride. Here, we draw upon the example of Hannah and Will's persistence through the pain they confronted. They, like each of us, entered intimate circles of relationship (acquaintance, lover, friend, spouse, etc.) and acted as if each one would endure, unchanged, forever. Complaisance lulls us into the belief that an intimate relationship will never end. However, the natural progression of life's events, from cradle to grave, reveals that these relationships are dynamic: They are born, they change, and they die. Moreover, when we enter an intimate relationship it gives life only to the extent that we are able to be open to the breaking or death of that relationship. This is the paradox of relational spirituality. In this chapter we explore how openness to the creative potential of suffering can help promote awareness of a deeper reality by pressuring us to put forth the effort to love others while also remaining open to the suffering at hand.

Chapter 3, "Obedience to an Interior Vocation," addresses a basic feature of the spirituality of relationship, specifically, that authentic intimacy does not impede, but can facilitate the processes of becoming a unique individual, which is known as individuation. In this chapter, students of spirituality will also find traditional themes such as gentleness, quiet, solitude, aloneness, and awareness. In this chapter, though, these themes are explored in the context of relationship. The reader will also find those themes that facilitate a communal experience, themes such as play and gregariousness, but these too are explored in regard to how they can facilitate individual discovery within the intimacy of relationship. In this chapter Simone Weil's concept of "essential vocation" is studied in light of the mutuality of authentic intimacy.[3] The spiritual concern for discovering the person we are called to be is explored in the context of formation, understood as co-formation.

Chapter 4, "A Passion for Reform," addresses the experience of dispossession and some of the relational tools that can be used to promote this experience. "Objectivity" is presented as the outcome of the relational equivalent of the spiritual practice of detachment. The experience of anger is also considered in its potential to help promote the relational objectivity needed for personal integrity. Here, three basic dimensions of anger are explored as a means of confronting those false identities that are inspired by pride and the smug arrogance we experience when we live with the attitude of complaisance. We explore what can happen if we live with the freedom of an anger that is creative. And we discuss an anger that can become a means of promoting "dispossession" and personal integrity, one that is also in the service of the experience of relational intimacy.

The last two chapters invite the reader to step back and take a more comprehensive look at the experience of intimacy as we move across the horizon of human relating from adolescence to mature adulthood. Research in the area of development is currently demonstrating that human life unfolds in distinct though overlapping phases.[4] The experience of relational intimacy admits no exception to the principles that contemporary investigations address.

During our search for intimacy we each appear, regardless of vocation, to undergo an *infatuation* phase, that is, we look at our respective worlds with eyes of romantic, but somewhat narcissistic, idealism. This falling-in-love phase usually incorporates a period of anxious searching for some one, some thing, or some place that will satisfy our heart's desire. Regardless of our way of life, when we do find what appears to be the answer to our heart's desire, we engage in rituals of courtship. The infatuation phase in the development of intimacy incorporates courtship and the early years in the formation of our public vocation. The movement from infatuation to courtship is like the shift from being a postulant to entering a period of being a novice. Here we develop some degree of proficiency with our chosen estate. During the courtship phase we also slip beyond the anxious idealizing of infatuation and take on a vision of things that is more objective and aware.

During the next period, we enter the phase of *personal profession*, when we become adept at being individuals with a point of view. This usually encompasses the era of middle adulthood. Here we gain wisdom and begin to emerge as beings who can inhabit a more individual and personal vision of self and other. In this period, our attempts at intimate relating still feature a fair amount of fumbling about. The narcissistic idealizing that is part of infatuation does not disappear all at once, but persists in periodically impeding our relational life well beyond mid-life. During this middle period we are, however, much more personal and proficient.

Next there is the phase of *espousal* when we are in a period of being somewhat more "objective," authentic, and compassionate in our manner of relating. The unfolding of each phase of relational intimacy, though, is not without pain. And in this third phase our attitude toward suffering becomes critical.

Chapter 5, "The Ascetics of Intimacy," addresses the crucial importance of suffering as it occurs in the unfolding phases of our relational life. During this reflection we retrace some of the steps taken during Hannah and Will's life together. Two distinct attitudes toward suffering are explained. One leads to a proud but unredeemed and unconverted brokenness, and the other promotes the humility that can emerge for a life of faith when we allow ourselves to undergo the suffering that is experienced when an intimate relationship is broken and the associated relational identity dies.

Chapter 6, "Intimate Circles," is also an overview of the life of relational intimacy. Again, the three phases in the life of intimacy are addressed. However, in this chapter we illustrate what happens when the suffering we encounter, as we experience human relating, is greeted with that openhearted stance promoted by a life of faith. Viewed from the perspective of a *creative* approach to suffering, the life of relational intimacy begins to take on a cast that resembles the three nights of faith addressed by St. John of the Cross: night of *senses*, night of *spirit*, and night of *soul*.

The way our intimate life unfolds does not necessarily guarantee that we will be privileged to undergo the spiritual adventure of the dark nights in the life of faith. Consequently, the reader should exercise caution in interpreting what seem to be corresponding phases of our relational life. However, with this caution in mind, we can identify the transformations which *might* occur for people of faith. Thus, three distinct moments are identified in the life of intimacy as it unfolds for people of faith.

In a relational journey sustained by a willingness to be open to the creative possibilities of suffering, these moments are: *awareness,* (personal) *integrity,* and the moment when as individuals we see one another with the awareness of compassion, which we call *presence.* These three moments are presented as the transformations that take place as we pass through the three developmental phases of the journey of relational intimacy: infatuation, personal profession, espousal. We develop an *attitude of awareness* when we can accept responsibility for the distortions we impose on self and other when we are infatuated. We develop an *attitude of integrity* when we can be who we are as individuals. We develop an *attitude of presence* when we can be tolerant and compassionate toward others. (See Figure 1 on page 11.)

The development of these three attitudes is presented as the transcendent possibilities that evolve on the journey of intimacy *if* we are open to the creative possibilities of negative experience. Thus, we employ the construct of a vertical ascent to illustrate the departure from the ordinary progression across the horizon of everyday relating. This is done in part to assist the reader in discerning that in the journey toward a loving response one need not always look beyond the simple acts of everyday relating to find the transcendent dimension. It is on the horizon of everyday experience that we initiate the adventure of intimacy and begin the vertical ascent toward holiness. There is in each of us the God who calls Self back to Self through the adventure of intimacy.

I hope the reader will be able to draw guidance for this

journey of ascendance to which we are all called. I am equally hopeful that in getting acquainted with the life of Hannah and Will Greaves you might gain a deeper understanding of the transcendent possibility to be found on your own intimate journey. And I hope, too, that you know or will meet people who are formed in the discipline of simplicity and openness to suffering required for the adventure of intimacy.

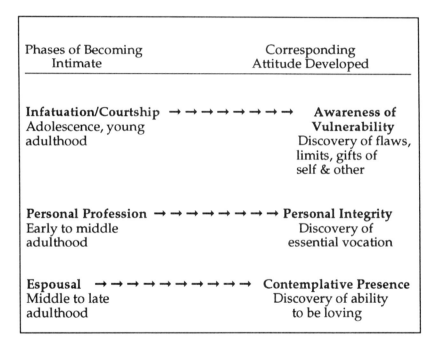

Phases of Becoming Intimate	Corresponding Attitude Developed
Infatuation/Courtship → → → → → → → → Adolescence, young adulthood	**Awareness of Vulnerability** Discovery of flaws, limits, gifts of self & other
Personal Profession → → → → → → → → Early to middle adulthood	**Personal Integrity** Discovery of essential vocation
Espousal → → → → → → → → → → Middle to late adulthood	**Contemplative Presence** Discovery of ability to be loving

Figure 1—Growth & Development of Relational Spirituality

You can get caught holding one end of a love
when your father drops and your mother
. . . and your friend blotted out, gone
. . . you reel out loves long line alone,
stripped like a live wire
. . . loosed in space to longing and grief. . . .

—Annie Dillard, *Holy the Firm*

The Adventure
of Intimacy

It may seem odd to begin a study of intimacy with a poem of suffering, but those who have actively pursued the intimate life will understand, because they have learned that suffering is the midwife of intimacy, its facilitator, its promoter, its John the Baptizer. The wisdom of this insight is slow in coming, but the seekers of intimacy realize both the cost and the joy of achieving it. My grandparents, Hannah and Will Greaves, knew; I saw them live from this knowledge throughout that part of their life I was privileged to share.

The intimate look Hannah and Will would exchange has

been a haunting memory, especially since his wake when she looked tenderly upon his silent face and wept. The intimacy they learned to share was visible even in death. I had seen that look many times while he was still alive. Sometimes it would appear following an argument, although, generally, not until a truce of some sort had been realized. More often than not, the appearance of this tender, intimate look was unpredictable. One day I saw it while he was peeking through the neck of a tee shirt that was hung upon his nose, making him look rather helpless and comic.

Will had arthritis. Toward the end of his life he sometimes required her help to get dressed. On this particular day, his pride at needing help apparently got in the way; an offensive remark he made caused her to interrupt the task. His arms were left dangling helplessly in the air, his head poked halfway through the opening. His large English nose was covered like a Muslim bride's. He was sputtering in anger; his pride wounded. At the moment I arrived, she saw the outcome of her work and began to giggle. In her laughing eyes, he saw the absurdity of his position. In the midst of his anger, he too began to laugh. Then I saw that wonderful, wise, playful, and tender look. She, too, is gone now. Their legacy to our family is that warm and wonderful look so generously bequeathed to each of us. But their legacy also includes how they managed to develop the ability to be free in their vision of each other.

It has been almost two decades since I have seen and talked with Hannah and Will. Still, I am haunted by the memory of what I observed. The scientist in me wants to understand how such a look is possible for him, for her, between the two. The child I was also desires to be with them once more and to understand more deeply all that they tried to convey. So, I begin this study of intimacy by turning once more to those who taught me first.

Intimacy: Celebrating the Birth of Self

In adolescence there are hungry looks exchanged that are full of the urgency of expectation. In the final phase of their life together, neither Hannah or Will would have had much patience with such a look; it would have been a distraction from the playful tenderness they enjoyed. They would have seen the adoring look of romance as an illusion, as manipulation; the urgent need of infatuated love would have been perceived as an imposition. The look they had finally mastered could dwell upon the other. It did not penetrate the reality of the other—it caressed it. Theirs was a look that could center attention on the other without needing to be the center of the other's attention.

Infatuation is love's novitiate, but it is full of dreams and insistent expectations. When Hannah and Will looked intimately at each other, it bore faint resemblance to the awkward intensity of beginners. Their look was fully professed. The illusion of love's idyll had been converted. The tension of love's novitiate had been displaced by something much more liberating and comfortable. Life had intervened to soften and relax their exchange; a patina of care had replaced the glare of an infatuated look. Upon each face a look of resignation now appeared, not the resignation of despair, but of acceptance. In some mysterious way, their moments of intimate exchange also revealed the price each had paid in undergoing the conversion of infatuated desire. Romantics may resent that statement. Yet, the intimate witness of Hannah and Will was an indictment of the infatuated urgency of youth.

The romantic look of youth does violence to authentic human intimacy. It seeks to devour, to absorb, to fuse with the beloved. Hannah and Will had lived through love's novitiate. Each knew and remembered the poverty of spirit imposed by the romantic illusion of perfection. Each had known the urgent desire to be seen, known, accepted by the other as the one who would fulfill all dreams and mend all broken hearts. Hannah knew the suffering of infatuated love's disappointment when the beloved's incapacity to satisfy our dreams becomes visible. Both had come to understand that the object of human affection has limits, weaknesses, imperfections. Each had suffered through the pain that love's urgent longing inflicts when human need seeks to find fulfillment through a human other.

At times Will displayed annoyance when she did not discern what he was seeking; the reverse was also true. Each could dismiss the other with an unkind remark, yet, despite the pain, they would persist in their effort to relate. Over the course of their lives, Hannah and Will learned that when we seek something from the other we are momentarily aware of our poverty and our need to be completed. They also learned that in such moments of poverty we must restrain pride and chasten the urgency of need.

Infatuated lovers are rarely as unkind as Hannah or Will could be to each other. Generally the wounds young lovers inflict are directed to those outside the circle, until they begin to fall out of love and seek revenge for the disappointment they experience. Hannah and Will could inflict a different kind of pain. Young lovers are disappointed when the other will not play a desired role; Hannah and Will could wound out of a vision of reality. Each was committed to inviting the other to get beyond the inauthentic dreams of adolescent desire.

Revealing a genuine need to another is an extraordinary risk. Failure to discern the other person's need or to speak directly to a flaw can cause considerable pain and disappointment. Hannah and Will learned to make the choices that enabled each to live their daily disappointments openly. Eventually, they were able to tolerate the pain with forebearance and good humor; this had not always been the case.

As a child I had sometimes heard their rows and wondered if the relationship would survive. At times I feared I would lose both; I feared the moments of angry exchange. I did not understand the forces of transformation at work within each. It is only now that I am beginning to understand that the power to wound is part of the price we must be willing to pay if we are to become intimate. It is only now after hours of dialogue with my family that I have a modest awareness of what Hannah and Will may have dreamed about as a young couple and how they each had changed.

They were not unusual or out of the ordinary as young adults. We can surmise that when they fell in love, awareness of the other's faults would have been threatening. I am sure they were no exception. In their later years, the look I observed them exchange could be characterized as having a hint of celebration, not the pride of conquest, but the realization that the arrogance of adolescent dreams had been chastened. Infatuated lovers are not able to admit the imperfections of the beloved to conscious awareness. The look of adolescent romance is also unbalanced: The beloved is "perfect"; the lover is "unworthy." The adoration is unfocused and unreal. The Hannah and Will I knew could look at each other and celebrate the pleasure and privilege of being attended to. They could also express disappointment of what the other could not perform or be. By the time I came along, they had long since abandoned the need to make the other perfect. They could look, see, laugh, and give birth to something special: their self, a self rooted in a vision of reality.

Intimacy: Forming and Living Two Dreams

Hannah and Will were married sixty-five years. Over that span of time, they shared many dreams; some were realistic, some were not. There were, however, two prominent dreams that they, like all of us, had to address. The first was the personal or formative dream that incorporates ultimate personal aspiration; it is the dream of who and what I can become. The second was the dream promoted by infatuated need; in the area of relationship this involves who and what I expect the other to be for me. In each of these primary formative dreams, the power of imagination is involved.[1] Both dreams affect what I intend to become as person.[2] In the first, Will and Hannah each had to discern the false from the actual possibilities in their lives. As it is with all people, these two dreams were brought into their relationship. Thus, their journey into the realm of intimacy was a discerning process between actual and unreal possibilities that touched each joyfully and painfully. Sometimes the dreams were inspired; sometimes they reflected illusions of self-gratification. It is inevitable that our infatuated dreams will fail. It is equally inevitable that we will impose our dreams on others in the form of expectation.

To understand the power a formative dream can have upon relationship, it is important to consider the larger context of our lives.[3] For the aspirations and inspiration we bring into relationship are not entirely of our own invention.[4]

In 1903, when Will emigrated from the English midlands to the factories of upstate New York, he was only eighteen years old. This fresh, young, innocent nation roared with the energy of adolescent enthusiasm; so did Will. A few years later when he returned to England, where he met and courted Hannah, the dreams inspired by America would persist. In 1924, with a young wife and four children in tow, he would return to pursue his dream of the "good life" in America. Will's adventures were in the service of his personal, formative dream.

When Will finally retired, he was almost eighty. He and Hannah owned a run-down frame house without central heat and sorely in need of paint. The house even sagged a bit, and water for bathing had to be heated on the kitchen stove.

He still maintained a garden for exercise and food. On occasion he would supplement their groceries by fishing. Hunting had been abandoned years before because his knees were too arthritic to tolerate the walking required. He did not drive or own a car. The only means of personal transportation he had ever enjoyed had been a bicycle. He had generally walked when he was able. If travel was necessary, he went by bus. The frustration and economic disappointment promoted by several wars, a worldwide depression, and several smaller ones that economists call "recession" had put him out of work often enough to keep them poor. Life, in the material sense, had been harsh for Will. By the time of his retirement, the American Dream had faded from memory. According to Levinson, the dreams of youth rarely become the reality of old age.[5] In Will's case, the American Dream became a disappointment.

Hannah also had her struggle with a personal formative dream. Her father had been a man of means. In her struggle to feed, clothe, and shelter seven children on Will's meager salary as an industrial laborer, she could privately nurse the hope of realizing her inheritance. The reality of her life was in sharp contrast to her aspiration of wealth. Eventually, she was able to develop and maintain some sense of perspective. With their second- and first-grade educations, she would learn what to expect of the culture. Years of working and cleaning for others of higher estate would eventually teach her the value of the education she lacked. Nonetheless, her personal formative dream, like Will's, would also intrude itself on her relational life.

Hannah and Will were poor. Life had conspired to administer something that a holy vow could only approximate: poverty. However, their struggle was not one of coping with the despair of shattered dreams. Although they suffered, toward the end of their life together they learned not to entertain despair for long. In time, they found that something

Thomas Merton calls "this little kernel of gold," this "spark of the soul" that is our "true" and "authentic" self, our "being."[6] The discovery of this dimension of human existence emerged from a long and painful process of confronting the personal *and* infatuated dreams of each.

Suffering: Companion on the Journey of Intimacy

The harshness of poverty can mortify and humiliate. In a materially-oriented culture the negative experience of being deprived is to be avoided. Neither Hannah nor Will ever gave court to poverty openly, willingly. In fact, she often spent her spare dimes playing "numbers" long before the State of New York made the practice legal. Yet, they did not get trapped by the experience of being poor. Somehow, particularly in their final years, each had been made free by the harshness of life. At the end, each would look back and weep at some of the agonies endured. They did not escape the pain of life's imperfection or injustice, but each learned to celebrate the moments of joy in a way that put them beyond the clutch of despair. This was a direct result of how they had learned to confront their dreams and expectations.

For people of faith, suffering does not lead to affliction and despair; it becomes a companion enabling them to strip away the illusion of a false dream. At times, suffering must silently accompany us through the grief of disappointment before we can experience a deeper sense of fulfillment. Sometimes we do not get what we want in order to realize what we need. This insight is difficult to comprehend when we see pain on the face of someone we love and are moved to try and join them in an intimacy of consolation in order to take the pain away. I recall my own discomfort when I saw the sadness that silently crept into Hannah's eyes whenever she spoke of her mother's death. On those occasions Will would quietly wait for the moment to pass or he would distract her with a warm and playful tease. But he would not try to take the pain away.

As a child I had only heard the more romantic features of the story. My maternal great-grandmother, Phoebe Jane Martin, had been a servant on the estate of a wealthy family. My great-grandfather, Thomas Browning, had belonged to a family of successful solicitors whom we have always believed lived in one of the "posh" sections of Lymm, England. From the elder Mr. Browning's perspective, Phoebe Jane's was an inappropriate estate. Consequently, Thomas and Phoebe Jane conducted their romance in secret, but she appears to have been a determined young woman: They eloped and were promptly disowned. Subsequently, the elder Mr. Browning seems to have had a change of disposition. On February 11, 1889, a marriage settlement was arranged. As part of the settlement, the Brownings established a lifetime trust out of the Manchester Branch of the Provincial Bank of England. Today, assuming prudent investments at a moderate rate of return, the trust would have had an approximate net worth of $1,225,000.[7] The pain that crept across Hannah's face could still reflect the urgent longings of an infatuated dream well into the middle of her life.

Hannah's personal, formative dream of the good life in America was, in part, a hope founded on reality. Such, however, is the stuff of Edwardian romance. Except, this romance was real and it formed an integral part of Hannah's formative dream. This feature of her dream significantly affected the process of becoming intimate with Will; it was a part of her formation story and became the occasion for considerable pain. For Hannah, as it does for each of us, an infatuated dream always spills over and affects how we relate to others. How we cope with the spillover affects our experience of intimacy.

There were times when the story of Phoebe and Thomas was rarely told in the Greaves house. During those periods,

Hannah made allusions to painful experiences that were mysteriously attached to any reference of England. Sometimes in anger she would reprove Will with the reminder that *her* father had been a "gentleman!" Will would walk away, properly chastised. He would not remain "in his place" for long. Eventually he would return, wag his finger in proud defiance, and declare that *her* father had been a "bum!" At times she would continue the argument, but more often than not, Will's rejoinder would achieve immediate victory: She would burst into tears.

I was an adolescent before I would learn that young Mr. Browning, this mysterious "gentleman," my great-grandfather, had disappeared under cruel and very painful circumstances, requiring Phoebe and six-year-old Hannah to face life essentially alone. The trust established for the young Brownings would continue until Phoebe's death; the halo of memory surrounding the trust, along with Hannah's attachment to her "gentleman" father, would linger considerably longer, affecting her aspirations of herself and her expectations of Will. Will would even be required to exorcise the spirits of her past *and* the mythical inheritance. But at the point of Phoebe's death, Hannah's personal and relational formative dreams seemed to have become hopelessly intertwined, where they festered to promote expectations far beyond Will's capacity to deliver. It would take years for the urgency of her romantic expectations to be tamed by the process of resignation, a process that requires openness to pain. It would also take years to develop the discipline of simplicity required to let go of the past.

The years following their emigration from England were hard on Hannah and Will and their family. Three more children were born, including twins. Eventually, the Edwardian romance of Phoebe and Thomas, Hannah's parents, became an occasional story told to the younger children. It would lie dormant, only occasionally finding its way into an argument between Hannah and Will. In 1934 it would once again be thrust painfully into the middle of their lives: Hannah would hear the news of her mother's death. After considerable debate, it was decided she would return to England, leaving the responsibility for the three younger children in the hands of Will, who was ably assisted by his four eldest children: Bill, Elsie, Hilda, and Rose. They survived one another's care until Hannah's sad return some eighteen months later. She had attempted in vain to satisfy her adolescent dream of recovering her inheritance. In the course of time she would be required to accept the fact that this dimension of her dream would have to die if her and Will's relationship was going to survive.

The story is told that friends of her parents', the Holloways, owners of a coal company, had offered the services of their barrister to assist in the recovery of the considerable money. It was a hard-fought campaign. In the end Hannah had to be persuaded to let go. The Browning family was too powerful. The financial stakes were high, but she had lost. Her dream of affluence for her family in America was relinquished with considerable reluctance. This dimension of her personal formative dream had come to a bitter and disappointing end, and, in 1935, she returned to America. In her possession was the only inheritance she would ever receive: a shawl and a snuff box. Her children would have to find the "good life" in America by some other means.

Will also had come to invest in that piece of Hannah's dream, although not by a free and conscious choice. The settlement papers, executed by Edward Eustance, a trustee of her parents' estate, were allowed to gather dust, but for Hannah the pain of disappointment would linger for a very long time. At that point in Hannah and Will's life, the primary relational issue was clear: They must face the disappointment and return to the task of learning how to get along. This aspect of their journey would prove to be an adventure of a different sort. Hannah would learn to become "rich" through radically different means than that inspired by her romantic dream of being an heiress.

We all remember Hannah as a joyous adventurer who could join any excursion and transform the event into a celebration. She was also a very charitable person. During the 1940s she was active in the U.S.O. as well as in her church and community. Always, she gave generously of her time and energy, often ministering to the sick in her community by preparing meals from her own kitchen. With their very limited resources, many poor and not-so-poor neighbors were fed or nursed back to health by meals taken from the family larder. Will bore her charitable efforts with quiet good humor. "If she heard someone were hungry," he would say, "she'll pick the gold out of her teeth to buy 'em a bit of bread." He would say this with astonishment. "That's the God's truth, she would!"

Will learned to be very affirming of her efforts to be of service. He knew it was based on what she heard in church and on her nature as a person. He was not an ungenerous or unkind man. He was stoic, hard-working, generally reserved in his judgments, but sensitive to the severe pain contained within Hannah's memories of England and her infatuated dream of being rich. Supportive as he was of her style of living, he would tease her about trying to be "Mrs. Rockefeller," his playfulness betraying a hint of sarcasm. But in a moment when his pride was wounded, he could trade upon the intimacy they shared by calling her father a "bum." He seemed to intuit what T.S. Eliot conveyed in his poem "Burnt Norton": that we are made vulnerable in time-present and time-future by the intrusion of time-past.[8] Will had shared in the pain of her past when her infatuated dream was in full flower and at times had been its victim. He knew he could be impeded by the past; he could understand how Hannah's romantic dream could interfere with the "little grain of gold" that was her "being."[9] With an unkind remark, he could inflict the pain of personal poverty with the skill of a Zen master. He seemed to comprehend that her dream of wealth could promote a deeper poverty than the one they shared. He knew it could rob her of the very identity he had come to adore. Will was very well aware that suffering is a companion on the journey of intimacy.

Pride: Investing in a False Identity

It is a given that we will invest in an identity inspired by pride. Sometimes, if only for a moment, our investment in that identity will be revealed by the anger or disappointment of those we love. We often act surprised or hurt when an identity we have carefully constructed in private is brought into the open. Often it is one that has already seeped into our heart and assumed silent possession. Generally, this process of formation is seen by others who share the intimate relationships we have developed; they know our secret selves long before we are able to acknowledge their existence. Neither Hannah nor Will was an exception to this principle. Indeed, it was often the basis for his dismissal of her father as a "bum." The remark, in truth, probably had nothing to do with Mr. Browning, but it did reflect the pain Will had to endure because of Hannah's adolescent dream of becoming an heiress.

Often, our secret identity, though privately held, seems intensely important, having been forged out of a mixture of expectation, need, and reality. Such a hidden identity can silently wrap itself around our heart and rob us of the energy to relate to a deeper, truer identity. Hannah had a personal dream inspired by the wealth she hoped to receive. In clinging to her dream, she did not see that it failed to provide her with the freedom to be herself. When her dream-self was exposed or threatened, she, like Will, could live from resentment and inflict pain on the perpetrator. Will harbored the belief inspired by an infatuated dream that he, not her aspiration of wealth, should be at the center of her life. This was his formation dream. His dream-self was equally false. For the absolute center of each and every intimate relationship can only be inhabited by a being who does not always satisfy our whims but does provide the ultimate fulfillment, when we become the person we are truly called to be.

There are hidden, secret places at the center of our lives to which our dreams and the false selves they inspire cannot gain access. Hannah's dream of being an heiress had been privately nursed and supported by a reality that combined to assume the force of an identity, an ego-self. When we stand in an imagined reality and expect those we love to take it seriously—to the point of paying homage—it is inevitable that this false identity will come under attack by people of integrity. Those who really care do not have a choice. Faith, Merton teaches, embraces a deeper, truer reality which will obtain.[10] Faith embraces the reality of a more profound self than that dictated by need or the expectations promoted by our dreams. This "self" made real by faith is the person familiar to those who share our circles of intimacy, but this deeper, truer self is not born without suffering or pain. In discovering this self, the pain we experience is born of our struggle to be freed from the enslavement that occurs when we cling to our dreams; it is the pain that attends the birth process of becoming authentic. Bernard Boelen tells us this process never stops.[11]

Pride, however, can impede the birth of self. Our dreams, both personal and relational, are formed in part by a pride that eventually creates a false identity. Merton proposes that this "false self" be dispossessed.[12] If we are to be free, the dreams of youth must be seen as false—even if they are realized. The truth of this mysterious paradox is revealed only within the intimate circle that can be formed within a relationship. Dispossession is possible only when those who see our inauthentic selves have the courage to challenge us to let go of what we cling to. This is the mystery and challenge of relationship. It also demonstrates the transformative power that can unfold within a relational circle of intimacy.

Intimacy: A Story of Choice

On the day I saw Will helplessly caught by his tee shirt, his pride had been as hobbled as by any action Hannah might perform. When I walked through the door, I had no idea I was about to witness a moment of dispossession, one that had been practiced whenever need arose. Nor had I any idea that the power of transformation could be as simple and swift. Hannah facilitated the transition from pride's fury to freedom's joy by a special kind of laughter. She did not laugh at Will, but, having seen the result of her own behavior, she laughed at herself and invited him to do the same. Her laughter did not contain ridicule; she was not rubbing his nose in his pride. She was being playful. She issued an invitation, one she had received many times before. He was able to accept it because she had allowed him to be free by not making his pride the object of derision.

Meister Eckhart teaches that when the soul laughs at God and God laughs back, the Trinity is born.[13] Will and Hannah were able to give birth to the Trinity within the circle of their relationship, and they had performed this ritual often before. When both saw the result of their behavior, they surrendered to a creative force beyond their pride, one they were intimately familiar with. They were able to make the choice to be free from the restraining power of pride in order that each might once again adore what was genuine and liberating in the other; this is the ethical choice that renders authenticity and integrity to an intimate moment. It was a choice exercised repeatedly through their lives, especially in the final phase of their relationship.

Freedom is the incarnation of hope within a circle of intimacy. In the arena of relationship, pride incarnates the slavery imposed by illusion and makes us impose unreal expectations on another. When I walked through the door, I saw each make the choice to be free. It was also a choice to be intimate. Each had seen their respective foolishness and made a choice to abandon pride. When Will surrendered, his laughter was an acknowledgment of vulnerability. In that instance he was indeed dependent on Hannah. For a brief moment he had refused to acknowledge his dependence. She had reacted by mobilizing her pride. He would soon learn who needed whom! His comic pose was not staged for effect; it merely happened. When she saw his predicament, she also saw his pride. Her laughter could not be directed at him. She could laugh only at herself. Her freedom invited him to do the same. When he chose to abandon his pride, he saw and accepted his vulnerability. He saw the gift she had become for him and he laughed. He laughed and his spirit was once more made free. He laughed and once more recovered a deeper, truer identity, one not of his making, but one that contained him, revealed him, allowed him to burst forth and personalize the room. Hannah did the same. Then that wonderful look emerged, that look that embraced pain and joy, poverty and gift, triumph and surrender, past and future. It was the look of a dispossessed self celebrating the fullness of life in all its adventure and simplicity.

It had not always been this way. It had required effort to move beyond their pride and the false expectations imposed upon each other. I can only guess at the myriad events that enabled Hannah and Will to let go of their expectations and unfulfilled dreams, romantic as they may have been. There is seduction, distraction, illusion, and lies at the center of our personal and relational dreams. There is also a seed of truth.

In the title of his story, "In Dreams Begin Responsibilities," Delmore Schwartz speaks to this initiation into life proclaimed by our dreams.[14] Hannah had a personal dream; so did Will. The dreams might have ended more favorably; they did not. Each worked to bring the dream to fruition. At times each imposed their personal and relational dreams upon the other; each failed. Together they had to face and resolve those aspects of their dreams that were personally and mutually destructive.

The story of their intimate adventure is one that tells how they gave birth to the seed of truth contained within their dreams and how they dispossessed all that was false. Hannah and Will's story is a love story in the deepest sense. It is a story of the agony and ecstasy of the intimate adventure that is life. It is a story that incorporates the wholeness of being and the brokenness that accompanies the adventure of intimacy. It is a story of wealth and of economic poverty, but also one of inner richness and poverty of spirit. It is a story of the process we must all endure if the journey to be intimate is also one that serves our truest, deepest selves.

Chapter 2

At the still point of the turning world.
Neither flesh nor fleshless;
Neither from nor towards;
at the still point there the dance is.

—T.S. Eliot, "Burnt Norton"

Slow paced I come
Yielding by inches.
And yet, oh Lord, and yet,
Oh Lord, let not likeness fool me again.

—C.S. Lewis, "Sweet Desire"

A Journey Across the Horizon of Relationship

In the pursuit of intimacy it seems inevitable we will suffer. It also seems inevitable we will learn caution. We yield to the invitation to be intimate, but only by inches. In our search for the still point we do not want to experience the pain of being fooled or the embarrassment of being foolish. So we distort reality and create illusions in the false belief that by living in the castles of our imagination we are safe.

Adrian van Kaam, Thomas Merton, and before them, St. Augustine and St. John of the Cross invite us to remember that we have both an openness to reality and a propensity for distortion; they tell us that we must lay claim to both.[1] Yet, in the process of searching for intimacy, it seems inevitable that we become victims of our natural inclination toward distortion and self-deception. Will was seduced by the American Dream; Hannah, by her dream of being an heiress. These seductions are a manifestation of the power of pride, which makes us act as if our imaginary castles are real and permanent fixtures in the landscape of our everyday lives.

The more common and daily occurrence is the illusion of permanence promoted by the phenomenon of *complaisance*. The messages of complaisance are instructions dictated by pride. It colludes with pride to create a desire for those warm and cozy little corners in our lives that make us feel secure. Complaisance also makes us impose our dreams on others in the form of expectation.

It is natural to believe that our personal security can be realized without pain. The insight of St. John of the Cross, however, is in sharp contrast to the illusions inspired by complaisance; he pointedly teaches that the peace of a "stilled house" is realized only after we journey through a "dark night."[2] Judith Viorst shares something of this vision in her book, *Necessary Losses*.[3] Does the protagonist of Lewis's poem "Sweet Desire" know this as well? Is he telling us we cannot dance at Eliot's "still point" unless we are prepared to pass through the darkness and pain created, in part, by our own pride? Must we suffer "necessary losses" before we find the peace-filled permanence we seek?

Intimacy: A Dance Through Many Circles

The formative dream inspired by infatuation is an attempt to get free of the slavery of complaisance; it initiates the journey toward a loving response. Infatuation launches our pursuit of authentic human intimacy. The journey of intimacy could also be called a dance through many circles within which we witness the formation of relationships with a specific set of expectations: chum, friend, lover, spouse, parent, etc. It is a journey of brokenness as relationsips end and continual emergence as new ones are born. Guides along the way—such as Daniel Levinson, Judith Viorst, Harriet Goldhor Lerner,[4] and those voices mentioned above—tell us that we must pass through a succession of intimate circles, each of which gets broken and must be relinquished before we can move on. They also teach that the suffering of a broken relationship, when integrated, promotes growth toward the wholeness of being.

The succession of intimate circles of relationship are familiar; they move across an emotional spectrum from distance to closeness. Initially, there is the warm, protective intimacy a child knows with its parents, the intimacy of kinship with siblings, relatives. Then there are the intimate circles one creates with those outside the family: neighbors, pals, associates, friends, best friends, lovers, a panoply of relationship forming a parade that marches across our lives from cradle to grave. If we are fortunate, a number of people enter our lives and are willing to dwell with us for a time.

Hannah and Will were indeed fortunate. The long line of mourners who formed a queue of respect at the funeral of each provides ample evidence. The mourning bench of every funeral home also demonstrates another reality: Each relationship we encounter on the journey of intimacy inevitably gets broken. These are the moments in life when the parade comes to a grinding halt. Then we all become like children: restless, impatient, eager to get the thing going again because we cannot tolerate either the pain of being or of waiting. On the journey of intimacy, our hearts are made restless by the harsh reality of life.

Complaisance: Clinging to the Past

Hannah was an only child. Her life unfolded against a background of Edwardian romance. She knew the warm, intensely private, and protective intimacy that can exist between a mother and daughter. She knew the adoration a child can experience toward a father, particularly one whose style and bearing were in such sharp contrast to the neighbors of industrial Langly, where they lived. Her identity in this small, misfit family inscribed itself deeply in young Hannah's conscious mind. Although she was only six years old when her family tragically dissolved, her identity with Phoebe Jane and Thomas was clear, distinct, and endured throughout her life. Indeed, if not for the active and somewhat forceful intervention of three thoroughly Americanized daughters, her youngest daughter would not have been named Joan![5]

The expectations of relationship wrap themselves around our hearts quietly, but very tightly. At times they are the silent dictators that give our affective lives shape, form, and direction. They often stipulate what gets spoken and how it is expressed. Fidelity, or perhaps "fealty," dictates what is "speakable." Loyalty to our secret inner identities also puts us in conflict, at times moving us to wound the people we care for. Because of our pride, the "unspeakable" at times gets spoken! Our friend, for example, expresses what we have decided to ignore through mutual collusion, which hides the truth. Sometimes the betrayal is in service of the relationship, sometimes not. Certainly, Will was wounded by Hannah's comparison to the first man of her dreams, her father. Will's retaliation was clearly the reaction of wounded pride, but it was more than mere narcissism.

Narcissus, the beautiful young man in classical mythology who became intensely enamored of his own reflection in a spring, could not respond to the adoration he evoked, and in the end invented a substitute self to mitigate the pain of being alone.[6] Will, on the other hand, had found a partner from whom he could receive and toward whom he could direct his adoration. At times, when he issued a retort, it was an attempt to free Hannah from an "inappropriate" attachment. However, at times his retorts were also an attempt to clear the way for him to reign, in order that he might dance with her all alone. He had not reckoned with the phenomenon of complaisance, which instructs us that once we enter an intimate circle, we generally insist that it remain intact. Regardless of intention, life does not bow to the proud demand of human desire. Thomas, her father, was gone; Hannah had to let go.

Inevitably, life forces us to move through one relationship to the next in the parade of human development, but there is a liberating spirit that accompanies every authentic circle of intimacy. It will not let us remain forever attached to any given relationship, although we inevitably try to fool ourselves into believing that this is false doctrine. On the other hand, complaisance is a quiet and insidious despot, demanding that we believe every relationship is permanent, but all dictatorships must face the risk of being overthrown. Expectations that compete must be transformed if any vocational commitment is to survive. Neither convent, hermitage, nor hearth escapes the need for a relational reform, but the ghosts that haunt every intimate relationship must be exorcised before the transformation can occur. However, pride does not readily yield to reality. It invades our imagination, making us believe we must cling to every relationship. Complaisance would have us dig our heels in and steadfastly refuse to let go of the past.

At the beginning of their relational journey, Hannah and Will participated in the courtship dance of lovers. By the middle of their relational life, they were able to journey side by side as friends. When Will died, their relational identity underwent yet another transformation. She became known as "Will's Widow." The journey of intimacy is an inexorable sequence of broken circles of relationship followed by the struggle of adapting to a new relationship and a new identity. Confronting the new identity and letting go of the past is painful, but it must be accepted or we cannot move on. If we are not open to the pain of dispossession, the ghosts will rule our lives.

Relationships offer the security of an identity; the names conferred because of the intimacy (mother, spouse, friend, etc.) seem as timeless and unchanging as a granite monument. The assigned title circumscribes a world of meaning shared by those who occupy the circle. Once we enter, the expectations implied by the title seem fixed and predetermined; certain horizons of possibility emerge; sometimes these expectations are not so much known as intuited; we seem to know, automatically, that a friend does not speak with the freedom of a lover, or that a colleague does not speak with the personal authority of a friend. This is the natural work of pride invading our imagination, circumscribing our freedom and our limits. Gradually, we are able to move in familiarity with what is expected, permitted, tolerated. Unwittingly and inevitably, we become familiar and complacent. We readily embrace each relational identity conferred as if it were both a badge of honor and the thread of life. We are creatures subject to the forces of need and habit; we forget that in order to participate in the fullness of love we must be free. Pride and the action of complaisance make us resist freedom; we do what is expected. And in the end, we cling to dreams and dead relationships.

When a relationship ends, the parade of life may grind to an abrupt halt, but it will always resume. However, the voice of pride tells us to resist any interruption. We are easily seduced. Pride, however, is blind to the outcome of its own actions. For when we suffer the loss of a relational identity, the pain is deep, even if ignored. Complaisance wants us to avoid or deny pain, relinquish our freedom, and become a slave, but relationships always get broken and the gaps that are created will not close, despite our posturing and pretense. Broken relationships inevitably become holes in our life. Complaisance makes us create illusions that force us to believe that life is a seamless garment, a constant thread that never changes, never breaks. However, "breaks" in our relational lives do occur and become "holes," which in turn become "graves." It is inevitable.

Hope: Formed in the Darkness of a Circle

On March 3, 1975, Will died. Toward the end of his life, we sometimes referred to him as "the old man." It was an identity of endearment used by virtually everyone he knew, including Hannah. It was, however, not a name we called him face to face. Individually, he was known as "Dad," "Grampa," or "Will," sometimes "Willy," but only rarely; for most who knew him respected him. People who were intimate with Will knew the silence he carried and addressed him with a kind of homey reverence.

When we spoke of him privately as "the old man," we were really addressing our history and the part he had played in our formation; we were giving testimony to his place and presence in our lives. We were also being influenced by images of permanence promoted by complaisance. We derived a measure of comfort in the expression. We could declare that someone had prepared the way to help us realize the place we now occupied. We were not orphaned; God's promise to Isaiah had been fulfilled in our family.[7]

Unfortunately, the pride of complaisance was also whispering its instruction. When prompted by complaisance, we called Will "the old man," which was our way of hiding in a dusty little corner to avoid our own mortality. It was as if we were saying he had *always* been in our lives; he (and we!) would go on forever. Hannah had come to know the lie of that illusion. She had seen the gaps of many broken relationships. She knew that the relationships we forge tightly always open and form holes in our lives. She had experienced many a hole in her life as it deepened through the pain of grief to become a grave. The wisdom of authentic intimacy had taught her that the formation function we serve for each other is also in service of a "dark night."[8] Hannah understood that these moments of darkness are necessary on the journey toward the ultimate peace we seek. She understood that hope is always formed in the darkness of a relational circle of intimacy.

Intimacy: A Struggle for Awareness

Will and Hannah's life together included a marriage of sixty-five years and friendships that endured about as long. During their span of life, each learned a valuable lesson. It was a lesson of harmonious co-existence; the wonder of intimacy that life offers can live alongside the deception we create. "Likeness" can and will "fool" us, and the "still point" will persist. If we are faithful to the darkness, dawn will come, but the horizon of hope will not appear unless the disruption to our lives created by a broken relationship is integrated into the fabric of life. The holes in our lives can enrich us, but only when accepted will we gain access to their hidden wealth. What is the secret? By the time of Will's death, Hannah knew and she encouraged us to delve into its mystery. She encouraged us to let go of our expectations and to be aware, to *take notice* of others; she also knew that in this contemplative act we become vulnerable.

Ortega instructs us that "taking notice" is the first moment of love. He observes:

. . . this taking notice is nothing other than a concentration of attention upon a person, thanks to which the latter stands out and is elevated above the common plane. Such favor in attention knows nothing yet of love but is the preliminary condition. . . .[9]

Awareness is not reserved for others only, but must also include self; moreover, it must be tolerant before a relationship can give birth to an experience of intimacy. Awareness leads to seeing and includes the possibility of learning that we can be deceptive and deceived. Acknowledging that we have a propensity for distortion *and* clarity can eventually promote playful acceptance of self and other. It happened to Hannah and to Will. Only when we are able to accept responsibility for the action of our pride and the natural movement toward self-deception can we yield that final inch that puts us at the center of an intimate circle, at the "still point" where "the dance" is. Before we arrive at the center, where there is only the moment of stillness and celebration, the road is difficult. Pride and the action of complaisance do not want us to acknowledge intimacy as a struggle. It wants our presence to life to stay at the level of dream. The self of complaisance must be dispossessed. It must be evicted from the central and controlling place it holds in our relational lives. Before we can inhabit our truest, deepest center, the one that gives birth to authentic intimacy, we must suffer the loss of pride and the death of those desires that make us collude to keep truth hidden.

Hannah took notice of Will. At his wake I recall hearing her speak of his eccentricities. I was surprised, confused, and sometimes shocked by her revelations. How could she look at him with such tenderness while he lay in his coffin and then speak of his odd behavior? I thought it callously disrespectful, a betrayal of his memory. I was very disappointed. Arrogantly, I had attributed her behavior to "grief." I was wrong. *It was love.* It was love founded on awareness. Hannah was not only aware of our propensity to be fooled and be self-deceptive, she was also aware of our inclination toward being foolish by trying to deny reality. She and Will had lived through the dream-phase of life. She knew Will in his humanness. She could stare at him lovingly and celebrate the entirety, the wholeness of his existence. She no longer had to supplement her witness with a dream.

In this "taking notice," we are contemplative, if only for an instant. Here we grasp Eckhart's vision: When we see and laugh at the absurdity of our existence we are born in God.[10] When we dispossess the self, which Merton calls the "false self," the self of illusion, we are able to yield that final inch and "receive the glory of God into ourselves. . . ."[11] When we acknowledge pride and the action of the false self of complaisance, we are free.

Hannah knew we must first undergo what Johannes Metz refers to as our "poverty of spirit," before we are able to dance at the "still point" and be filled with the luxurious rest that is God.[12] Hannah loved Will with that holy love that enables us to see, know, accept, understand, tolerate all those intimate moments that flow from "bearing witness."[13] She knew that when we are aware and open to our own foolish self of deception, we can be rewarded by the gift of being accepted, understood, and known by others. John Dunne writes: ". . . if I am known I am accessible. . . ."[14] The path to this accessibility is through an opening that can be created by our "consent to self-surrender."[15] The self-surrender that leads to self-acceptance provides access to a relational circle of depth and substance that is much more nourishing than our dreams; the parameter of this circle forms the horizon of a peace-filled world and gives birth to the experience of intimacy.

A relational world of substance and depth is always rimmed by a horizon of hope. When we persist in a circle of intimacy, we become familiar with each other; in awareness we become *known* to each other. Hannah *knew* Will. Will *knew* Hannah. By the end of their life together, Hannah and Will knew that they were known by the other. They had participated in a relational unity, an experience that John Dunne describes as the from and of and toward: ". . . the with me, before me, behind me, in me, beneath me, above me, on my right, on my left. . . ."[16] They had experienced that unity of loving and knowing we call intimacy, an experience realized through a struggle to be aware, an experience realized when the real presence of witness dispossesses the imagined witness of the self of complaisance. At the end of their lives, they knew that intimacy is a struggle for awareness and they could immerse themselves in awareness.

Love: An Effort and an Outcome

Hannah attained wisdom. She had arrived at the understanding that pride, which promotes our natural inclination toward distortion, constitutes the absurdity of human existence. She knew that pride prevents us from being open and accessible to self and other. There were moments when she could blame Will for her troubles. She could entertain thoughts full of self-pity that would, on occasion, become an outward grumble: "If only you had not taken me from my mother . . . if only you had not had this dream." I believe she also knew such solitary thoughts were a distortion of the kind that lead to isolation, loss of hope, and eventually to resentment.

Born on December 9, 1888, Hannah was eighty-six when Will died. She had realized an age when wisdom had dispossessed the urgency of expectation. During this phase on the journey of intimacy she was not as easily seduced by complaisance. Her awareness of Will, with his gifts and eccentricities, had enabled her to see, hear, and speak from her heart. John Dunne refers to this kind of presence as "wisdom."[17] She could see beyond the expectations painted by dreams, could see beyond the pain of disappointment. She could accept the pain that emerges when someone in an intimate circle fails to fulfill all that the particular relational title implies by way of expectation. She could look laughingly or tenderly upon Will's face and see with eyes of friendship and of wisdom. She had been dispossessed of the illusion of her infatuated dream, a dream that dictated who he *should* be for her. In her mind she had granted him the right to be himself. In her struggle to be intimate she had discovered that love is an effort *and* an outcome. Even when his life was over, she could persist in the effort. She could look at his cold, dead face with eyes of warmth and tenderness. She could see with eyes of awareness rooted in love.

Hannah had taken time to become aware of Will, but she had not learned "to see" entirely on her own. Bit by bit the lesson had unfolded. With each broken relationship, she had come to understand, she had experienced love's pressure, which manifests itself at every pause in the parade. Will's death fulfilled and broke the bonds of matrimony. It was not the only broken relationship she had known; there had been many. With each pause in the parade, she had learned once more how to put forth the effort to be intimate and new relationships were born. With each pause, the pressure of love encouraged her to see.

Will had been an agent in this enterprise. His long, solitary walks had enabled him to draw upon an inner resource. Together they learned the importance of putting forth the effort to be intimate. Each knew their vowed commitment required work if the marriage was to be kept intact. The pause in their parade presented by each broken relationship, regardless of the circumstance, had enabled them to see each other with a clarity of vision made possible by love's pressure, a pressure that teaches us to see each other whole. Neither had ever read Rilke, but they knew

. . . once the realization is accepted that even between the *closest* human beings infinite distances continue to exist, a wonderful living side by side can grow up, if they succeed in loving the distance between them which makes it possible for each to see the other whole against the sky.[18]

Hannah and Will had undergone the pain of broken relationship and had learned to see with eyes of wisdom. In the face of what they saw, each had yielded to love's pressure. They had learned to see with eyes of wholeness because each had helped the other to incarnate their personal vision of others with a sense of compassion. With their vision obscured by the illusions formed by pride, they had entered a relationship called marriage. Each emerged as an individual who could put forth the effort to see with eyes of love. At the end, each could "see" the other "whole against the sky."[19] They could see each other "whole" because they had accepted the inevitable pain of harsh moments encountered on the horizon of everyday relating.

. . . When I talk about solitude I am really talking . . . about making space for that intense, hungry face at the window, starved cat, starved person. It is making space to be there.

—May Sarton, *Journal of a Solitude*

. . . The joy that playful gentleness brings is not merely the joy of passing consolation. . . .

—Adrian van Kaam, *Spirituality and the Gentle Life*

Obedience to an Interior Vocation

When Will died, Hannah was alone. All seven of her children had married. Four of them continued to reside in the village where Hannah and Will had spent the bulk of their lives; the rest within an afternoon's drive. She had numerous grandchildren. In the urban sprawl of most cities of the northeastern United States, Green Island, New York, is an anomaly, a small, self-contained village, essentially untouched by the surrounding metropolitan area. For Hannah, its provincial boundaries all but guaranteed a steady flow of visitors through her home.

In their sixty-five years of marriage, their longest period of separation occurred when her mother died and she had returned to England to try to recover the estate. Now, with Will's death, she was alone. On the surface she appeared to be struggling with the experience of being by herself. The struggle, though, was not with being alone. She was very lonely and hungry for Will's company, but she was able to stand up under the experience. She and Will had realized that special kind of aloneness essential for the experience of intimacy. Each knew the value of silence and solitude; each understood that aloneness is as necessary for intimacy as air for breathing.

Vocation: Responding to a Fullness Shared

In a reflection on Louis Lavelle's *Le Mal et La Souffrance,* May Sarton asserts the belief "that solitude is one of the ways toward communion."[1] She tells us that Lavelle describes solitude as promoting the feeling of "presence in oneself of a power that cannot act, but which, as soon as it is able to, obliges me to realize myself by multiplying my relations with myself and with all human beings. . . ."[2] Hannah and Will understood the generosity of spirit that flows from solitude.

Sixteen months after Will's funeral, Hannah died, on July 10, 1976. Our family had grown quite large and we were aware of her gregariousness and natural generosity, but no one was prepared for the outpouring of affection from so many beyond our immediate family. Hannah had indeed "multiplied her relations," and it seemed she had done this with "all human beings" who were now appearing *en masse* at the wake!

McNulty's funeral parlor was stretched beyond capacity, with the line of mourners seemingly endless. People shook hands and in various ways touched, hugged, or clutched at one another in gestures of greeting, sadness, and desperation. Interminable introductions were made to people I had once known, people whose awkwardness indicated that they, too, had been chopped down by Hannah's death. Each mourner would search the face of one family member or another. Each wanted to remember or be remembered. They would reminisce, perhaps recalling a funny incident. We would laugh only to be enveloped by an awkward silence, wondering if it were appropriate to feel so light when surrounded by such heaviness.

Sometimes, generally after a reminiscence, I would look around the funeral parlor. It was decorated in colors suggesting subdued elegance. Walls, floor, appointments, flowers, the dull bronze casket—throughout the room, the color, scent, and fabric all spoke of silence. There was the constant shuffle, murmur, and muffled sobbing of mourners trying hard to conform to the decor. Then there were those bursts of laughter that could not be contained.

In some mysterious way, despite the awkwardness we felt, the crowds and bursts of laughter were acceptable. It seemed natural that Hannah would attract so much attention, natural that so many people would be undone by her death, natural that there were so many fond and funny memories that burst forth to contradict the decor. It all seemed natural, for in answering her vocation she stood witness to that fullness of presence we call life. It was a fullness she readily shared with others, "multiplying" her relations with everyone she met.

Marriage: Reconciling Opposites

In death, as it seemed throughout her life, Hannah appeared to have been surrounded by people. Family, members of her church, friends—she was always in a crowd of one kind or another. As a child, I had thought a week was not complete unless there was at least one gathering, no matter how brief, around Hannah and Will's dining room table. I had taken that image of them into much of my adult life.

It is only now, in dialogue and in retrospect, that other images, memories, experiences emerge that cast their relationship in a different light. In talking with members of my family, I have come to realize that if love is an effort, its effect radiated outward from both Hannah and Will. The effort was toward each other: Hannah toward Will, Will toward Hannah. The effect of their union also radiated outward, toward others. Ortega would have smiled in approval. For the direction of their love was a constant going forth toward others: continuous, fluid, constantly active; affecting Hannah, affecting Will; touching, enveloping others. The eddy created by their union was pampering, flattering, affirming to all who came in contact with it.[3] Even in discord, the effort of their mutual love was constantly at work. When they argued, those they loved would hope or pray for immediate reconciliation, in order to recover the effect of that outward, flowing love that seemed always to seep out of their union.

At Hannah's funeral, frequent comments were made about the comfortable intimacy she and Will had realized. They were perceived as being "very close." Hannah and Will were indeed close; however, they were quite independent of each other. She could enter a room and before she made it to the opposite door a party was in progress! Will was the more quiet participant in the union. Hannah could envelop herself in song; Will could do the same with silence. She was good at having fun. He was good at being quiet. More important, both could be in a room together and allow the other to do what each did best. Each could also imitate the other: Hannah could be silent, Will could initiate the fun; they balanced and complemented each other.

Intimacy: Presence Realized Through Struggle

The gift of letting the other be had not always been spontaneous; nor was it practiced flawlessly. There were moments when Hannah would be sitting in their front parlor enjoying an afternoon of silence. Will would arrive as if by preordained appointment and turn on the television, abruptly ending her journey into solitude. Occasionally her irritation would be revealed. At other times she would accept his insensitivity with quiet resignation. Sometimes it simply did not matter, for being alone was an option he generally respected. It was perfectly acceptable for her to withdraw from him; she could afford the same privilege.

The intimacy in Hannah and Will's marriage was formed out of a respectful witness to the personal and relational value of quiet, solitude, aloneness. The effect of these values crystallized within each in quite different ways. Their intimacy was such that each could go apart, then return to the relational union of work, play, or leisure. They could be alone, then enter the positive and affirming experiences of understanding or acceptance, or they could participate with gusto in the harsh moments offered by life. In separation they would gain the perspective needed for any given moment; in union they were free to work at promoting those essential, human experiences that sustain and reinforce the intimacy of relationship. Will could go apart and rediscover the wonder of being quiet. It had a formative impact on Hannah's gregariousness. Her gregariousness, in turn, connected his solitary style to herself, family, neighbor, and friend.

The effort of their life in common enriched each and radiated outward, touching others, inviting all to be at home in their presence. The realization of their "comfortable intimacy" did not miraculously appear; it evolved through a willingness to struggle.

Silence: Will's Personal Vocation

On the journey of relationship, silence and gregariousness are polarities that must be reconciled within each of us, regardless of our public vocation. According to Charles Maes, silence is intended to separate us from the world of everyday involvement. The effects of silence are recognized by monasticism and psychoanalysis. The former recognizes its role of facilitating access to our deepest source of interior nourishment; the latter, its role of facilitating access to those troubles in our lives not immediately available to conscious awareness.[4]

The silence of a psychoanalyst creates a favorable atmosphere for the re-emergence of those difficulties in our lives that have been buried in the past. In our relational life the pride of expectation will provide fertile ground for our imagination such that our unsolved difficulties in life can continue to assert their power and presence in the form of disappointment, anger, anxiety, sadness, etc. The past can continue to live itself out in the present with the assistance of our pride with its insistent demand for satisfaction in the name of fairness.

Will had never been the subject of analysis, but he had learned how to cope with these inner forces. On his long, solitary walks he had learned to listen. In silence, it might be said, he had undergone a formation in the ancient art of recollection. He had learned how to listen to his own inner ache and be soothed by a comfort deeper yet within. By the end of his life, he could listen to Hannah speak of her father and playfully tease about her superiority. "Yes," he would say, "your father was a gentleman," and if he sensed she had not seen the urchin in his eye, he would remind her of her superior education: He had completed first grade; she had finished second!

In and through silence, Will had learned how to separate himself from the unrealistic expectations created by his adolescent dreams. On his long walks, he had learned the external dimensions of silence. He had learned the playfulness of spirit that emerges from being recollected and aware. Hannah also had been instrumental on his journey. She bore witness with him in his public vocation. She also helped shape and direct the discovery of what Simone Weil calls "essential vocation."[5]

It has been more than forty years, but I can still recall accompanying him on one of his walks. It was intended to be a hunting trip into "the Pines," a little strip of forest lying to the north of Green Island on the west bank of the Hudson River. It was autumn. The month escapes my memory, but the day remains as clear as if it had just occurred.

The air that day was dry, crisp. The bright sun, its rays piercing the foliage, created an eerie display. This little patch of forest promised adventure. At the outset I got caught in the excitement of being allowed to participate in the secret, manly event. Proudly, I tromped along recklessly letting my feet fall where they would, ignoring what might be underfoot. I was ignorant of the crescendo of noise that can be created in the forest by the snap of a dry twig. I was completely oblivious that my lack of discipline was keeping many a warren intact. Will was direct, but tolerant in his instruction. Toward the end of the day, I was beginning to follow his example, though I was unaware that the effect of my inexperience already had cancelled the original intent. There would be no rabbit for the stew from our expedition!

I have never learned to really care for hunting, but it did not seem to matter much to Will, for he taught something much more valuable on that excursion. He was offering instruction on the value of quiet places, something my own father would later reinforce by his example. We walked for a long time that day, Will and I. Toward day's end, I managed to perform what was expected: I walked in silence and awareness through the woods. I think Will was happy at what transpired.

On the way home he talked about a previous excursion in which a rabbit he was stalking got pinioned between the exposed roots of two trees. He spoke of the incident with wonder and amazement that a creature of instinct could get caught in such a predicament. To my surprise, he related his story as if he had no choice except to release his prey. He told this story with humor, gentleness, and wonder. I now realize he was revealing that his hunting walks always had a quiet, gentle, deeper purpose, one that had been fulfilled on that day of our walk. His story was, I think, intended to speak to a child's concern for the future. He sensed I was both disappointed at the failure of our hunt and worried that my inexperience would remove me from future consideration.

It turned out not to be the case. In the years ahead there were many walks, but that day was special, for on that day he was telling his story in the spirit of the Baal-Shem, the saintly Jewish storytellers and mystics of central Europe. Will's story was not unlike a teaching-tale in the ancient tradition. He was revealing something secret and mysterious, telling a story gently and in tenderness. He was teaching of wonder and intimacy, of the surprise that is the reward of walking in silence. He was offering direction—gentle, but direct and firm—to a novice on the discipline of silence. He was demonstrating how to be aware. He was giving witness to the importance of wonder. He was disclosing something he had learned: the vulnerability, peace, and mystery that emerges through the practice of silence and solitude. He was teaching recollection as a means of communion with something deeper yet within, something to be shared with others.

He was revealing his own transformation, and he had the wisdom to know it was not merely his own. As a young child, I had known Will's rough style of play. At times I was fearful. I also had observed some of the less than tender interactions between himself and Hannah. And I saw the transformation in gentleness that occurred.

By the world's standard, Will was not an educated man. Yet, intuitively he knew of *hesed* and *shekina*.[6] He knew the reciprocity between creation and Creator. He understood that silence affords access to the "indwelling" *(shekina)*. He had a firm grasp on the insight that God's loving kindness *(hesed)* must be greeted with a devoted and open-hearted love. Eventually, I would learn that on a solitary walk our dreams and sometimes not too playful fantasy can co-mingle with the silence of the world and be tamed. In Will's private little strip of forest, he had known the quiet ecstasy of wonder, awe, and mystery, but it was not the only schoolroom he would know. Life with Hannah and seven children also gave instruction that those moments of silent, burning joy must be balanced by *avoda*, the wonder that derives from service and devotion.[7]

In the course of his life, Will learned of the transformation in gentleness brought about by the acceptance of pain. Adrian van Kaam tells us, ". . . divine gentility is the secret at the root of a playful life that shares in the playfulness of the Eternal Word. . . ."[8] Hannah's gregariousness had provided something more than just a practical balance in Will's life. His practice of silence had taught him that recollection is essential in order to listen to life. Her sense of being playful taught him how to get released from the natural, interior divisiveness that spontaneously occurs when our pride is wounded. She had taught him not to evict the gentle mystery from his heart by refusing to be kind and open-hearted with others. On his long walks, he, in turn, was able to gain a deeper sense of her witness. He could walk in silence without getting lost within his heart. He may have learned of *hesed* and *shekina* in the Pines, but the discovery of his personal vocation had also been facilitated by Hannah's devotion, commitment, and natural gregariousness.

Where Hannah was caring, Will was firm. At times his firmness could move toward control and become oppressive.

At such moments the tension between them would be palpable, at times rather audible! "Bloody stubborn bugger," she would shout. At which point Will might begin a series of taunts, his Birmingham accent becoming just a bit more pronounced, while his regal, English nose would tilt upward at just the right imperial angle to intensify the aggravation. I cannot testify to the lengths to which his stubbornness might stretch, although I am told it had been quite formidable when he was young. By the time I happened on the scene in 1938, three of his children were married and had resources beyond his sphere of authority. I can only guess at the chastening effect this must have had. From the experience of my youth, I can testify that the interior wedding of firmness and gentleness was well beyond courtship.

On the day of our walk, I was ten. The rough man of my childhood who wanted to be playful was not the playful man of my youth who had to feign roughness. His silence had been important for the transformation; her playfulness appears also to have been of equal importance. The witness of her care was constantly at work attuning him to others, ever so finely, carefully, softening but not weakening him with a constant and gently flowing joy.

Play: Hannah's Personal Vocation

Where Will was firm and quiet, Hannah was gentle and joyful. Simply put, it was fun to be with her. She could make any event become a celebration. When she initiated an activity, everyone within earshot was drawn to participate. Everyone who knew her seemed to feel that the center of the universe was where Hannah cleaned the fish! Hers was a talent to be with others. His was a talent to be alone. In their final years, each realized that generosity of heart that enables us to share the specialness of our individual existence with others.

The marriage Hannah and Will enjoyed is testimony to Rahner's observation there is a "sacral secret at the heart of all play."[9] Thanks to Hannah, Will learned to share the secret; her playful spirit enabled him to gain access to its message. In his response to her, she discovered that play calls for silence and solitude. He discovered that without play silence can become dour, harsh, and mean. She discovered that without solitude play is frivolous and empty. Both discovered that solitude without the liberating joy of play becomes Narcissus at the pool: proud, angry, melancholic, desperate, and alone, a scorner of love, trapped in a solitary world with no one to love except oneself.[10] Will taught her that play without the gift of solitude is frivolous and makes a mockery of life. Hannah's gregarious nature kept Will from getting lost in the seriousness of his vocation of silence. Her sense of play fostered his freedom of discovery. Each learned from the other; each lovingly enriched, complemented, and balanced the other.

Hannah's playfulness created an atmosphere that permeated their home. As a child, I do not recall being aware of the conveniences they lacked; at a daily meal or a holiday their table spoke of abundance. A sense of fullness affected our perception of their tiny house, for it seemed as spacious as a football field. On a cool summer's eve, while Hannah and Will would visit on the front porch, the younger children would huddle together in the summer kitchen and toast marshmallows with a wooden match. Sometimes there would be a secret excursion to the cellar to check on the progress of Will's elderberry or dandelion wine. Their house held the promise of adventure. There were harsh moments, but they were like the lumps in Hannah's mashed potatoes: infrequent but digestible. The atmosphere of their home was provided by Hannah's playful, firm, and gentle disposition. Hers was a "playful seriousness, a gentle gravity."[11] Will had introduced the note of gravity; the gentle playfulness was her own.

In the course of their life, Will learned to take Hannah seriously. In the process, the roughness of his disposition had grown smooth, softened but not weakened by her sense of play. In a moment of conflict, she could interrupt her meal preparation, wave a spoon in his direction, and sputter in solemn anger. A moment later we would hear the wheeze of her laughter at his playful mockery. She would try to reclaim the dignity of her anger, but to no avail. She would appear to be undone by his attempt to imitate her playfulness, but his teasing had a deeper purpose. He had demonstrated that her playful spirit had indeed made an impact on his life. In the presence of such humility, she could not be bound by the arrogance of the absolutely just. Will understood this aspect of their commitment. He had learned his lesson well and could turn aside her wrath by a spontaneous witness to her playful spirit. "Yip! Yip! Yip! Yip!" he would respond, with that slightly tilted nose and ever-present "brummy" twang, revealing his origin in West Bromwich, England. History conveyed by intonation. Transgression accepted without apology. Peace restored with laughter. She could not endure in her demand that he apologize. For he had already responded to her request. He had told her by way of playful imitation that she had affected his life and he had changed.

Vocation: Public Witness and Interior Call

"The joy that playful gentleness brings is not merely the joy of passing consolation. Infused gentleness has permanency because it springs from my inner depths where the spirit dwells . . ." writes van Kaam.[12] Hannah and Will could dwell in different worlds. He could walk in solitude through the woods. She could sing and dance within a crowd. When together, their two worlds could intertwine. Each could challenge or invite the other. Together they were able to create a relational world that was flexible but firm, serious but fun.

Each held tenaciously to his and her exterior vocation. In the process Will was made gentle and Hannah was deepened: public witness promoting personal growth.

The development of their intimate union had not been smooth. There were occasional, possibly even frequent, lapses into gravity or avoidance, but neither remained trapped by the somber claim for justice made by pride. Hannah liberated Will from the egoism of a solitude that goes apart *from*, not *for*, others. Will liberated Hannah from the excessive frivolity and light-heartedness of play. He understood that play can turn frivolous and empty in its need to avoid the harshness of life. Each learned to take seriously the interior vocation of the other. Both learned to celebrate the essential simplicity that can and perhaps must accompany a life in common. Theirs was a life of poverty, but they were not impoverished; they were obedient, but not oppressed. In their marriage they were faithful to commitment, but each facilitated for the other the discovery of a personal vocation.

On December 25, 1909, Hannah and Will were married. The public identity created that day featured a circle of intimacy known publicly as marriage. One could argue that the public witness of their marriage vows only addressed one of the distinctly different avenues by which people profess to seek a meaningful direction for life. However, the relational witness of Hannah and Will also speaks to another dimension of human existence, one shared by all who seek intimacy. Theirs was a witness to Heidegger's insight that human presence is not merely spatial proximity, but the "being with" of mutuality.[13] Hannah and Will cared *for* and *about* each other; they were *there* for each other; each made room for the other. Together they learned to live a life founded upon *care, concern*, and *solicitude*.[14] Through awareness each learned to call the other into the fullness of being an original self.

Using his special gift for solitude, Will taught Hannah how to listen to the silence of the world. Through her special gift for play, Hannah taught Will how to dance and sing to the music he heard. In the process of relating, they sometimes stepped on each other's toes; yet, they kept their sense of humor while struggling to accept and integrate the pain. John Macquarrie reminds us that the human condition is shaped by the fact that we are a "fallen people."[15] For Hannah and Will, their fallenness became a pratfall in a live and sometimes comic production called life. Their witness went beyond the relational situation defined by marriage; it spoke to the universal response of one fallen human being responding to another. The witness of their life gives a resounding "yes" to the question Cain posed to Yahweh: "Am I my brother's keeper?"[16]

The experience of intimacy permeates all vocations. In homes, convents, monasteries, and rectories, various relational circles are formed to sustain the public witness of these different life forms. The witness of Hannah and Will clearly addresses those relationships involved in marriage: lover, spouse, parent, friend. Yet, their life together also speaks to another level of vocation, which St. John of the Cross implicates when he refers to the second night of the spiritual journey, the "night of spirit."[17] He teaches us that this second excursion into the "dark night" experience is darker than the previous "night of senses" in that it is illumined by interior, not exterior, structures.[18] Simone Weil proposes that such an interior experience is needed for the discovery of an interior disposition she calls "essential vocation."[19] Both St. John of the Cross and Simone Weil describe this spiritual night of faith as one in which everything is removed from both the intellect and the senses and we are alone; we are alone "in darkness," but "secure."[20]

Merton seems to amplify the observation, telling us that in the *night of faith* we as *person* are fortified by our "consent to receive the glory of God into ourselves" and thus become our "true self."[21] Hannah's fidelity to self and her commitment to Will enabled him to undergo this night of faith and emerge to become a unique *person*. On the road of self-discovery and self-emergence, she facilitated and supported him by her care and sense of play; he put forth the effort to do the same. The outcome of their mutual effort was the emergence of two distinct, *original* people who could enter the experience within relationship we call intimacy.

Yet, their life together as husband and wife speaks to a level of human commitment that extends beyond the horizon of public vocation; each was obedient to this higher, deeper level. Each became aware of an obligation to develop that special sense of individual presence that fosters intimacy. In developing their originality and independence each became free to exercise their sense of awareness; each served the other and became self-forgetful. In the process, each enabled the other to enter the personal, interior dimension of self-discovery.

Together, they were able to celebrate what they found, namely, that public vocation could also serve the discovery of personal vocation. In creating the space for the individual discovery of personal vocation, each also enriched the space where they dwelled together in public. On the journey of intimacy this reciprocal and paradoxical facet of their relationship was an important and connecting link between two distinct and different dimensions of their existence: the human and the transcendent. Hannah and Will explored both dimensions.[22] They made their personal discovery on the horizon of everyday relationship with each other and it enabled each to undergo the process of personal growth and transformation we call interior, or spiritual, growth. Along the way, they discovered each other in a different light; in the process each also discovered what van Kaam and Merton call our "original"[23] and "true self in God."[24] Their fidelity to ordinary life, where we meet each other as friend, lover, spouse, etc., also moved them into the transcendent dimension, where we encounter each other with a sense of reverence that enables us to see each other "whole against the sky."[25]

Hannah and Will's witness is a testimony that this personal, essential, individual, original, and unique "true self" is one whose discovery may be facilitated through a process that can only be called co-formation.[26] But while the mutuality that made this possible served as midwife, this "self," once born, was naturally drawn to share itself with others. Throughout the period I was privileged to share with them, this is exactly what each did. And in their sharing, the intimacy of their union had a profound effect on others, "multiplying" the relational circles of those they met over and over again!

In the next chapter we will examine some of the key features of the co-formation process. And we will learn how the birth of our interior, personal vocation makes it possible for our individual lives to be formed so that the transcendent can enrich the relationships we are called upon to form as we travel across the horizon of everyday life.

Chapter 4

Let us not malign our feelings
But lift them into the light of the spirit.
Instead of driving anger underground
Teach us to take its sting away.

—Adrian van Kaam, *Spirituality and the Gentle Life*

A Passion for Reform

Intimacy is an experience of being with others that involves closeness, physical or emotional. It is also an experience in which we must retain the freedom to be separate. The option to be alone is necessary if one is to discover the self of essential, or personal, vocation. Hannah and Will could be together and each could appreciate, respect, and support the other's need to be alone. Yet, the intimacy they shared was not merely an affirmation of individuality. Their love, faith, commitment, and self-discovery eventually brought them to a point where each could acknowledge the fundamental right of the other to exist; this was an essential feature of the love each held for the other. Each could be alone and discover something special deep within.

When they were together, they could draw upon this inner resource, stare in kindness, and behold the other with eyes that were reverently affectionate and respectfully objective. Each had arrived at a point where the picture held of the other was not clouded by illusion or maudlin sentiment. Each could see the gifts and flaws of the other. Each could look at the other and see with eyes that accepted the past, affirmed the present, and prepared for future possibilities.

Objectivity: A Relational Tool

The relational skill of seeing another person with eyes of tolerance, acceptance, and compassion is generally not the mode of everyday vision fostered and supported by our culture. Adrian van Kaam, John Macquarrie, and Bernard Boelen take this assertion a step further, suggesting that in our childhood we begin a cultural formation that is in service of distraction.[1] We are systematically taught not to see the frailty of our fallen human nature.[2] Culture teaches us to hide our imperfections and see through the eyes of illusion, not objectivity. By the time we attain adolescence, "objectivity" is understood as a cold, calculated, impersonal scientific term; it is not viewed as a relational tool that can respect and protect our essential frailty. It is rare for relational objectivity to be seen as inherently tolerant, compassionate, and accepting of human frailty. When it is rooted in integrity and compassion, objectivity can minimize the possibility that my attempts to establish intimacy with others will be based on the distortions inspired by the self of pride. When rooted in care, objectivity is the relational equivalent of holy detachment.

On their formation journey, Hannah and Will learned to see the reality of each other with a vision that incorporated flaws and imperfection. They were able to realize what Adrian van Kaam describes as the "natural rhythm between distance and encounter," the former required for relational objectivity, the latter for intimate relating.[3] Promoting the life-rhythms necessary for objectivity was an inherent part of the relational life of Hannah and Will.

The way Hannah and Will realized the life-giving possibilities of the rhythm of distance and encounter may have been thrust upon them by life's circumstances, the origins of which were buried in the past. However, their mastery of one of the primary relational tools required to develop the ability to be objective was readily understood by every member of our family. Hannah and Will had learned to fight! Each could get uproariously angry at the other. Their ability to mobilize this most tainted, sinful—and in the thinking of Carol Tavris, "misunderstood"—emotion would have inspired applause from Leslie Allen Paul and acclaim from John Osborne.[4]

Anger: An Ethical Emotion

Anger, as Hannah and Will expressed it, moved across a spectrum of feelings that included irritation, being sore, indignant, irate, mad, and furious! On very rare occasions they could express something resembling rage, but it stopped significantly short of wrath, probably due to the fact that each had too much respect for the divine. The freedom each displayed with this most tainted and misunderstood emotion also betrayed the significance that passion played in their life. It must quickly be added, however, that while their intimacy incorporated anger, it excluded hate.

I vividly recall the righteous sadness they spontaneously displayed when one of us expressed hatred. Neither Hannah nor Will could tolerate the movement of one human being against another. In anger or affection, they insisted, when you move toward others you must do so on their behalf. The anger each could express toward the other generally sought to reveal something, not inflict a wound or seek revenge. If it happened that one deliberately hurt the other, it was quickly recognized as a radical and unwelcomed departure from their usual mode of relating.

Hannah and Will had suffered many trials in their sixty-five years of marriage. Gradually, they arrived at the realization that love *and* hate are efforts constantly active in human relationship. As a mother, Hannah understood that love seeks to envelop others in a favorable atmosphere. She had not read Ortega, but she knew that "near or far, love is always endearing, flattering, affirmative, pampering."[5] Hannah had experienced a burning hatred toward her father's family when she was robbed of her inheritance and her dream. Will also had suffered the bitter disappointment that accompanies loss. At times, I observed in each the passion of an anger that sought to wound. I saw those brief flashes in each when I was a child; but they were very brief. My most vivid and compelling memory is of a curious kind of anger, one softened by love; it was the anger of two people constantly affected by the presssure of love.

Hannah and Will understood hatred as a passion that intends injury, destruction. They had seen the devastation that occurs when anger is unchecked and becomes hatred. They knew that hatred emerges from a pride that seeks to dominate others by first promoting disunity and discord. In the third and final phase of their relational journey, they were humble and could not participate in the self-idolatry that leads to isolation and the death of gentleness. On his long walks Will had experienced that creative isolation we call solitude, an experience of isolation which, unlike the aloneness of hatred, is the celebration of aloneness *freely* chosen. Through Hannah he had learned how to put his aloneness in the service of others. Will had a generosity of heart that hatred cannot afford. Despite a quiet, stoic appearance, his behavior in her presence validated an antipathy for the selfish isolation induced by pride.

When Will died, the intensity of Hannah's bereavement indicated that this was true for her as well. They could fight and not become isolated from each other. Theirs was an anger transformed by love, one dispossessed of the desire to destroy. In their struggle to relate, they learned that anger, repressed, would accumulate, grow beyond the original injury, and eventually explode against others. Each knew that the pride at the center of hatred does not grant the right of others to exist.

I cannot recall any display of emotion from either that even remotely suggested a desire to annihilate. They had learned to fight, but over the years they had learned to fight on behalf of something that transcended self-interest. The right of the other to exist was a fundamental feature of their love for each other; the ability to fight was in the service of the ethic of that love. It was a relational ethic, one always in the service of others.

Creative Anger: Vehicle for Reform

How had they developed this ability to fight? To approach this question, it is important to reflect on three dimensions of anger: ordinary anger, pathological anger, and a third I will refer to as *creative* anger.[6] We can dispense with pathological anger rather quickly, for their expression of anger did not appear to be in service of hidden or repressed motives; neither seemed to act as if they were trying to settle an old score with someone from the past. The past may have featured prominently at one point in their life, but the angry exchanges I observed, both as a child and adult, seemed to generally reflect a desire (albeit a somewhat heated desire) to change what was perceived as an unjust situation; this is ordinary, healthy anger.

The third kind of anger, creative anger, is similar to ordinary anger in form and expression; the difference is found in *perspective* and *application*. Creative anger is a passionate, emotional expression in service of reform. In the expression of ordinary anger, the individual perceives injustice and reacts out of the personal pain it creates. The expression of creative anger emerges from a similar perspective. The angry person's pain is still acknowledged, but in its expression a larger purpose is served. When Hannah and Will's anger was of the creative variety, it reflected a desire to maintain and enhance the gentle intimacy of their union. I vividly recall one such occasion. It was Christmas; logic and some detective work place it around 1949.

At this point in Hannah and Will's history, all but two children were married. In each household preparing for the celebration, there was the usual scurry of activity: pies, cakes, and cinnamon pinwheels to be prepared; chestnuts roasted, turkeys dressed, vegetables cleaned; relish and garnish; presents, tree, and table—all the trappings and trimmings that contribute to that wonderful Christmas aura and aroma. And the pudding? Ah, yes, plum pudding, always served at the very end of the meal when everything else had disappeared from the table.

Presenting the Christmas pudding had always been a special event; in some respects, it was even more eagerly awaited than the meal itself. With great ceremony, all of the lights would be extinguished, save those on the Christmas tree. A hush of anticipation would fall over each of us: A match was struck. A deep blue light appeared. At first a mere candlelight of flame was scarcely visible, delicate, flickering, barely alive. Then a great ball of radiant blue flame appeared; each face around the table became visible, bathed in the eerie blue light. Hearts filled, first with joy, then with an exquisite sadness as the flame gently licked the pudding and slowly disappeared—only to reappear first here, then there, dancing round and round the plate, teasing us, appearing, disappearing. The flame, continuing its feeble dance as if in response to our "oohs" and "ahs," finally vanishing into the void of a hushed silence as we stood around the table, quietly, expectantly, holding our breath, hoping for more. The silence was only an instant, but we were all held together by its spell. Something wonderful and mysterious had happened and we did not want it to end.

I recall that this particular Christmas had ended in the same, sweet, mystery, but along the way a great row had ensued. The details were somewhat hidden from us children both by the tinsel and wrapping and by the self-conscious adults who sought to maintain the magic of the day. However, we had caught sufficient glimpses of the fracas to clearly understand that something had been breached between Hannah and Will.

When dinner was finally served that day, Hannah's finger was wrapped in gauze. She had cut herself carving the turkey. Normally this was Will's chore, so I can assume either he had been preoccupied with visiting or had had a bit too much of the elderberry wine for which he had realized family fame. In any event, it seems harsh words had been exchanged, initiated by Hannah's desire to maintain the schedule and serve a piping hot meal.

The banquet had begun in uncomfortable silence, conversation being limited to the necessities of serving. Eventually, a more animated conversation developed, punctuated by an occasional cap-pistol exchange between the two antagonists. Sometimes the remark was ignored. Sometimes, it was met with a playful but irritated chiding by the other diners. Eventually, the dispute became absorbed into the celebration, not forgotten, but nudged aside by nostalgia and noisy enjoyment. But the angry remarks they exchanged during the meal served to reveal their formula for transforming the hatred of human pride into the anger of a loving relationship.

Before the Christmas meal had begun, Hannah and Will had enacted their particular version of Armageddon. During dinner their conflict had resolved itself into a more workable anger. Hannah was able to make known to Will: first, that she was angry; second, what he had done to provoke her anger; and third, what she expected him to do about it. The process was ordinary, healthy, direct, and very explicit. He did not have to guess at what went wrong. On subsequent occasions, I would observe that he could expend the same effort on her behalf.

Anger, for Hannah and Will, was a healthy, if somewhat uncomfortable, expression of their care for each other. Their care went beyond merely "taking notice."[7] It reflected the more fundamental relational sense of care as concern, interest, and solicitude.[8] They understood that their interest in each other had spawned a gentle intimacy that was at once both fragile and dynamic. Each possessed an intuitive awareness that pride can pose a threat to the frailty of intimate presence. Each knew that care must be continually served or pride would dominate their relational life.

Their anger, for all the discomfort it could produce, was a guardian of the delicate helplessness that lies at the core of intimacy. On that Christmas day, she had fought to protect this child of their union. She had sought to protect by way of *caring* confrontation. She could tell Will what had gone wrong and what she wanted him to do about it. She did not shriek, stomp, pout, or sulk. Perhaps at some point in their life such sullied expressions of anger had been possible, but on that Christmas day, something more than ordinary anger had taken place. Even now it is clear to me she experienced a desire to attack. Without equivocation, she intended to change something perceived as unjust, something that interfered with the wholeness (and perhaps holiness) of their commitment. She did not hide or repress the desire for attack. However, there was more to their anger than a corrective movement *against* each other. While their anger was an ordinary and healthy expression, it contained a *fourth* element, something more fundamental (indeed more *foundational*), to the *what, why,* and *remedy* of anger. This fourth element sent their anger beyond a merely destructive feeling to that emotional richness we call *passion;* this fourth element made their anger creative. It provided the heat, warmth, and eventual light whenever they underwent a night of conflict. This fourth element served as a bonding agent for the intimacy they shared. It was the *freedom* of creative anger that promoted a continual reform of the pride that deforms, distorts, and displaces gentleness.

Creative Anger: Passion with Perspective

Neither Hannah nor Will was intense in their political activity; though poor, they did not mobilize their energy in the direction of social change. George Orwell might have looked upon them as "proles"; Upton Sinclair would have been chagrined at their resignation to the social conditions that contributed to their poverty.[9] In the face of their work, my use of "passion" and "revolution" could easily evoke derision. Hannah and Will were, however, passionate revolutionaries. For each, in a profoundly quiet, simple way, was intent on stripping away the false and sham, all those counterfeit identities that mock integrity. When either was unfaithful to their deeper, truer self, the other invariably got angry. At such moments the other's anger revealed the passionate vision each possessed of their relationship. Theirs was a mutual and implicit understanding of what is essential in order to preserve and promote the intimacy of human existence. Theirs was a *passion with perspective.* Whenever either one perceived a threat to the intimacy of their relationship, it would initiate revolt, one in service of reform, not annihilation. All falseness and puffery had to be turned out of office at once! The genuine, authentic, and real had to be restored quickly and without the slightest dribble of explanation!

Freedom: Element of Transformation

During that infamous Christmas dinner, Will mocked her snaps of protest. However, he had failed to take stock of the loving and moral relational witness each had inspired in their children. The uninformed might be led to conclude that Will had been coerced into submission by Hannah and the celebrants. Not true! Will had responded to the fourth element of their anger: *freedom.* Both lived from an attitude inherently and deeply respectful of the other's freedom. Any remedy brought about by coercion might achieve an expedient truce, but would just as quickly be rejected. All those Christmas diners gathered around the table allowed themselves to see the pretense and harshness of Will's behavior. They also granted themselves the right to see the pride in the middle of Hannah's righteous insistence on the *absolute* truth of her point of view.

While each snapped, postured, or otherwise preened their wounded pride, the Christmas diners spontaneously assumed the posture of Robert Bolt's "common man."[10] It was our turn to witness to the integrity and compassion they had taught. The comments of the Christmas diners were nothing less than a mirror reflecting the integrity and authenticity of Hannah and Will's relationship. Their offspring had been formed in the principle that while truth can be firmly and passionately told, it must be answered only in freedom. The comments of the guests would reflect the only poverty Hannah and Will would ever really despise: the poverty of person that accompanies loss of integrity.

Through the eyes of the Christmas guests, Hannah and Will were able to see the caricature each had been drawing of the other. Each was thus able to reclaim with grace and wisdom a more balanced and objective vision of the other. Each had allowed the sting of anger to be felt, while being careful to withdraw the poison of hate. The anger revealed was palatable and never even came close to spoiling the Christmas pudding!

Passion: Fire of Conflict

What had happened? How was it possible for Hannah and Will to express that most dreadful of human emotions? How could they have grown in simplicity and gentleness and still have had such rows? The answers to these questions are found not only in the understanding of anger each had realized, but in their understanding of commitment. In assisting each other to discover the self of essential, or personal, vocation, they also assisted each other in dispossession of any false self that might emerge and interfere with a truer and more fundamental identity. They were committed to a journey of integrity and each encouraged the other to undergo continual renewal: renewal of self and of other. Indeed, they were committed to work on behalf of self and other. Each knew that one would not push the other beyond the boundary of what was possible. Each was also willing to put the other to the test. Each understood that in order to purge the false and artificial and give birth to a deeper, truer self, one sometimes had to undergo a baptism of fire. They had loved each other with sufficient passion that they were able and willing to ignite the fire of renewal by being angry.

Once upon a time, they met, fell in love, and got married. During all their years together, they transformed the circle of relationship called marriage into an intimate world in which many could participate. In the process, each arrived at the realization that a relational circle can be called by many different names. They learned that each identity had to be both validated and purged of pride. On their relational journey, they learned that the true had to be continually addressed, the false dispossessed. They learned that the force for renewal and reformation was a mutual devotion that embraced passion. They also learned that the journey of intimacy leads us into a world of passion where we can embrace the healing gentleness of *care* and the caring confrontation of anger.

Their life story is a formation story of relational intimacy.

It is a story that incorporated the pain of conflict, the wonder of self-discovery, and the celebration of reconciliation. It is a story filled with the fire of passion, which could illuminate their nights of conflict or bathe their family in the warm intimacy of a Christmas pudding. Theirs was a special kind of suffering: a caring and *creative* suffering. Their love for each other enabled them to grow beyond poverty and transform the harshness of everyday life into a quiet, rich, ascetic experience where each became a person of integrity, simplicity, and quiet faith, while the intimacy of their union grew in stature and depth.

One dark night
Fired with love's urgent longings
—Ah the sheer grace!—
I went out unseen
My House being now all stilled

—St. John of the Cross, *The Dark Night*

It is the heart that is not yet
Sure of its God that is afraid
To laugh in His presence

—George MacDonald, *Sir Gibbie*

The Ascetics of Intimacy

Darkness and laughter are both polarity and paradox on the journey of intimacy; resentment and pride are parallel possibilities. In an essay on his own rapid descent from a storybook life into brokenness and despair, F. Scott Fitzgerald writes:

Of course all life is a process of breaking down, but the big blows that do the dramatic side of the work—the big sudden blows that come, or seem to come, from outside—the ones you remember and blame things on and, in moments of weakness, tell your friends about, don't show their effect all at once. There is another sort of blow that comes from within—that you don't feel until it's too late to do anything about it, until you realize with finality that in some regard you will never be as good . . . again. The first sort of breakage seems to happen quick—the second kind happens almost without your knowing it but is realized suddenly indeed.[1]

As a young man Fitzgerald had perceived the harshness of life through eyes that did not find redeeming value in suffering. In his early adult life he thought the harsh blows of reality had to be met with a determination "to make them otherwise."[2] "Life," he believed, "was something you dominated if you were any good. . . ." It was something that "yielded easily to intelligence and effort. . . ."[3] "And then," he discloses, "ten years this side of forty-nine, I suddenly realized that I had prematurely cracked."[4] He had learned that in meeting the painful, agonizing moments of life, the self of pride and determined will can only bend so far; then we crack and watch in helpless, desperate resentment as the intimate relational rings we were determined to forge break apart. Hannah and Will had experienced the harsh blows of life but managed to avoid the devastating plunge into resentment and brokenness, which the force of Fitzgerald's will could not prevent.

Humility: Relishing the Joke of Our Existence

St. Teresa of Avila tells us of our need to be open, humble in the way we encounter life.[5] Van Kaam states: ". . . this openness should enable us to overcome our tendency to blow things out of proportion under the pressure of the pride-form of life." "Humility," he tells us, "tempers pride by humor."[6] It enables us to remain grounded. Fitzgerald took a determined stand toward life, lost his ground, and "cracked." Hannah and Will lost ground, materially, but they grew in freedom of spirit.

Hannah and Will were not spared the suffering of life. Yet, before being claimed by death, each realized an abiding peacefulness that was palpable and constant. Being in their presence was a refreshing and enjoyable experience, even under the most difficult circumstances. They had learned to meet life's difficult moments in simplicity and quiet faith without being broken or humiliated. I vividly recall an exchange I had with Hannah. I had telephoned to inform her of the birth of Kevin, our fifth child. At the time, I was in graduate school, a fact she and Will found puzzling. Both worried about our finances, often sending a few dollars "for the children" out of their meager resources:

"Gram, Carol had a boy."

"That's five, Tommy; you've more children than anyone else in this family."

"Oh, no I don't, Gram!"

"Who? Tell me, who has more?"

"You, Gram, you had seven."

"Oh!—yeah—I did. . . ."

At that point in our exchange she began to wheeze; Hannah's irrepressible laugh was about to burst forth: ". . . and I 'ad a good load of fun doin' the job too!"

Her worry and concern had moved her toward scolding, but she quickly saw the humor of the situation. She and Will had brought seven children into the world. In the process they had survived several wars; anxiously waited for sons and sons-in-law to return from combat; had survived a worldwide depression; in three separate tragedies had experienced the sudden, unexpected death of two grand-children and the joint death of two of Will's sisters in an automobile accident; experienced the deaths of parents, sons-in-law, and countless friends. Despite such tragedies, Hannah could face the dark moments of life and still relish the joke of her existence. Will could do the same. Both were humbled by life, but not broken or humiliated. Each managed to retain a sense of humor. Life's harsh moments never made them "crack."

Faith: The Necessary Patience

In order for the human journey to become spiritual, we must develop a sense of awe in the face of life's mystery, instructs van Kaam.[7] Following the path of Hannah and Will provides a glimpse of how this sensibility was formed in each. However, a note of caution is in order, for one might easily conclude that their story can offer guidance only to those who are married. While this may be essentially true, it is also patently false. The cruel moments of life are not selective; at some point in every life we are invited to participate in those dark nights that can give birth to the true self born of faith. We have a choice: Accept the pain and grow, or resist and crack.

Vladimir and Estragon, Beckett's clowns in the play *Waiting for Godot* find life humorous, but without meaning. They cannot perceive the mystery of suffering and so they are trapped in the anguish of despair; suicide seems the only option. Throughout the play, their humor remains as shallow and disconnected as their sense of suffering; and for them, Godot never arrives.[8]

The humor of Hannah and Will was full and rich. They knew, through faith, that the one we await has already arrived. They understood their God was present at each "blow," not as a malevolent being who made them suffer, but as a joyful, loving, supportive being who taught them not to take it seriously. "When God laughs at the soul and the soul laughs back to God," Meister Eckhart says, "the trinity is born."[9] The friendship and intimate communion they shared enabled each to face, accept, transcend, and share the pain and suffering of life and never lose perspective.

Hugo Rahner describes an authentic player as one who is earnest about life. He tells us that two essential features are known and held fervently by such a player. First, life has meaning; second, one's existence in creation is gift, not necessity.[10] Unlike Vladimir and Estragon, Hannah and Will found meaning in nurturing each other's sense of life as gift. Rahner is clear and unequivocal:

> ... these two pieces of knowledge reveal two aspects of our earthly life which the person who truly plays will never cease to be keenly aware of. The first is that existence is a joyful thing, because it is secure in God; the second, that it is also a tragic thing because freedom must always involve peril.[11]

Fitzgerald found that life's blows would not withstand his determined effort to reverse the process. He "cracked" under the strain imposed by his determined response to his wife Zelda's mental illness and his own decline. Vladimir and Estragon were perplexed by life's harshness. They could neither abide or understand any pain—either that of a shoe that was too tight, the pain of separation from each other, or the oozing sore on Lucky's neck. For them, as for Fitzgerald in his youth, pain and suffering did not make sense.

Hannah and Will were not literate in the complex problems of philosophy or theology, but they were in life experience. They readily understood the freedom and peril of existence. They could meet the agonizing moments of life with a sense of humor grounded in faith. They were not spared from suffering, but could meet it patiently with an openness of perspective developed out of participating in the challenge and mystery of encounter on the horizon of relationship. Each could meet life with a sense of play grounded in faith. Each believed in the existence of a benevolent presence who was always available to sustain them through the harshness. And they learned this lesson by cooperating with the ascetic process of everyday life, an ascetic that pursues people of faith from cradle to grave.

The dark agonies each had undergone prior to their first encounter had prepared them to be open and to persist. Their experiences of play had taught each to face both the victories and failures of life. Their moments of being alone had taught each the value of being recollected and aware. Fortified with the wisdom learned through these activities, each grew in humble simplicity. This quality, in turn, instructed each not to resist the dark moments that life inevitably would place in their paths. If the candle of hope were momentarily snuffed out, one or other would relight the wick. If either one put out the fragile flame by the puffery of pride's resentment, sparks would fly. Hopelessness simply was not to be tolerated. One way or another, peacefully or through a holy war, the flame of hope would remain lit.

Infatuation: Eyes So Full of Hope We Cannot See

On December 25, 1909, in a small church on Baptist End Lane, Oldbury Parish, West Bromwich District, Worcester County, England, John William Greaves, moulder from Halesowen Street, and Hannah Bently Browning, spinster, from Union Street, were married. She was an attractive woman. Her dark eyes, soft brown hair, and milk-white complexion had quickly captured young Will's attention. He was a ruggedly handsome young man, tall, slender, with the muscular good looks of an athlete. In his deep-set gray eyes

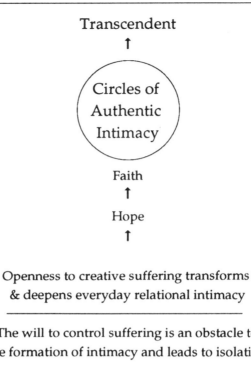

Transcendent

↑

Circles of
Authentic
Intimacy

Faith

↑

Hope

↑

Openness to creative suffering transforms
& deepens everyday relational intimacy

The will to control suffering is an obstacle to
the formation of intimacy and leads to isolation

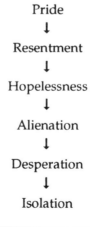

Pride
↓
Resentment
↓
Hopelessness
↓
Alienation
↓
Desperation
↓
Isolation

Figure 2— Formation Dynamics of Intimacy

and high cheekbones there was more than a hint of his Celtic ancestry. His smile was gentle, strong, and mysterious; it could summon images from the *gruagach*, the wizard-warrior of Celtic history. Hannah's face bore a look of gentility and care. She was not beautiful, but hers was a face that instantly evoked hospitality, warmth, and comfort.

It is the intertwining of appearance and hope that provides the playing field of human attraction. In our youth, dream commingles with need to ignite the fire of desire. The circles of intimacy we form on the horizon of everyday life are shaped by hunger and the false light of illusion. Those who are infatuated, then, should not be criticized for their inability to see with detachment. In their hunger for love, they seek perfection. When at last they find a loving other, the pain of loneliness makes them insist it must last forever.

When they married, Hannah was barely twenty, Will was twenty-four. When they met, each was a novice at falling-in-love. During youth the romantic illusions of love are intense and tend to linger through life. I can still recall the look that came over Hannah's face when she reminisced about their courtship. I could sense her adolescent belief that on that December 25, so very long ago, he was the Christmas gift offered by life. In his smile, she believed, she had found the answer to her past and the promise for her future.

Against a background of pain and disappointment, the urgency of infatuation tends to burn with greater intensity, enchantment–urgency, and desire; hunger and need are the alchemy of attraction. In our youth, love's urgent longing generally flares with intensity, enkindling hope, promising relief from a dark night of loneliness and pain; this was true for Hannah and for Will. However, we must remember that the "night of senses" in adolescent infatuation is more than the hunger for sexual expression; it is a promise of relief and a prelude to subsequent movements of spirit and soul—and it begins in darkness.[12] It is from out of this darkness that we gaze upon the faces of those we love and see the promise of relief. But its promise is one to which the beloved cannot respond until the imperfections of self *and* other *and* life are allowed access to the circle of intimacy each is trying hard to create.

Through the long history of their relational life, Hannah and Will would occupy a variety of intimate relationships: acquaintance, betrothed, spouse, lover, parent, friend. In the process, the fire of infatuated desire would touch every intimate circle eventually formed within their relational life, enabling each to become a person both passionate and playful. In the beginning, they were a couple made blind by love's urgency; at the end, each would become an individual who was able to see with loving awareness. In the beginning, as it is with everyone on the journey of vocation, they were made blind by hungry eyes too full of hope; at the end, the intense need within their hope was tempered by faith and each could see with graced detachment. Gradually, through each other, their pride was dispossessed by the gentleness of care and the earthy good humor that is humility. They were not broken by life's harsh blows, but came to gradually see and understand the creative possibilities found through suffering.

On the first leg of the journey we call vocation, pain tends to alter our perception of life. Before they met, Hannah and Will had been dealt those pain-filled moments we call reality. When she was barely six, she had suffered an abrupt and cruel separation from her "gentleman" father under mysterious and confusing circumstances. At eighteen, Will had pursued his dream to a new land only to have it snatched away before he was barely twenty-one by the sudden and unexpected death of his mother. For each, the wonder and promise of courtship would be played out against the painful backdrop of loneliness and loss. The first circle of intimacy they would enter together would be formed, in part, out of an attempt to mend the broken pieces of other relationships. Together they would learn to accept and integrate these shards of pain, but they would also be required to learn not to try to re-create the past.

When they met, Hannah and Will each brought the dark night of history into their first relational circle; each was too naive to realize that the mystery and challenge of encounter would transform the illusion of desire for what *was* into a wider, deeper vision of life. Through the other, each would be awakened to the meaning of life, and to the wonder and rapture of being alive. Their life together did indeed incorporate pain, but they never allowed suffering to become affliction. Dorothee Soëlle tells us that affliction is suffering without hope.[13] Estragon, Vladimir, and young Fitzgerald each were "afflicted." Hannah and Will received life's blows, too, but were empowered to respond by hope. It was not, however, an automatic disposition; it required hard work. Romance ignores the labor of encounter; love is aware of the work required. The transition from romantic distortion to love's awareness is clearly visible when we examine their courtship and early years of marriage.

Their life was not unusual, because we find suffering in every relationship. In their life, though, we observe how the discipline of simplicity is affected by the open-hearted disposition of humor. We discover that dispossession and detachment are made possible by pain. Indeed, we find in the gentle good humor of Hannah and Will an appreciation for the whole of life, an appreciation that enabled them to participate fully, even while undergoing the ascetic transformations promoted by pain.

Courtship: Invitation for Personal Emergence
I do not know all the details of Hannah and Will's courtship. I do know that Hannah first became aware of Will because of

Phase of Life	Corresponding Relational Attitude	Relational Structure
Infatuation/ Courtship Adolescence/ Young Adulthood →	Awareness of Vulnerability ←	**Intimacy of Senses** Witness of Invitation
Personal Profession Early to Middle Adulthood →	Personal Integrity ←	**Intimacy of Friendship** Witness of Personal Transformation
Espousal Middle to Late Adulthood →	Contemplative Presence ←	**Intimacy of Love** Witness of Personal Acceptance

Action of the life force of creative suffering promotes the attitudes essential for the growth & development of relational spirituality.

Figure 3—Growth & Development of Relational Spirituality

his skill as a football player. Will, the miner's son with the rough manners, had returned from America to assist his recently widowed father in caring for the remnants of his family. The death of his mother had been a shock, occurring as it did while he was so far from home pursuing the American Dream.

At that time in history, Langly was an industrial area. Film and photograph of Hannah and Will's England convey something dreadful and dreary of which Sergei Eisenstein's movie *Potemkin* or Robert Flaherty's documentaries may only be a modest exaggeration. Cities in the industrial English midlands were a noisy, smoky, greasy, hodge-podge of factories and row houses, not unlike the Pittsburgh of 1900. The horse cars that provided access to the rolling country hills must have been a tempting escape from the personal pain and dreary landscape Will experienced. Hannah's history brought its own share of pain into their courtship. But the challenge and mystery of first encounter always offers the promise of a wider, deeper vision of life for all who have the courage to participate and the willingness to endure. During the encounters of courtship, this enlarged, hopeful vision is found in the simple, concrete realities of everyday existence; it is manifest in how we see, smell, taste, touch, and hear a new world suddenly made visible through the other.

Hannah's mother had been in service to a wealthy family; her father had been raised in the English countryside. Will was a miner, foundryman, football player, and was unaccustomed to the quiet diversion of the English meadows. Life for him consisted of hard work and hard play. A pleasant horsecar ride next to his beloved Hannah; a leisurely stroll berry-picking, listening to the meadow birds; one of Hannah's picnic lunches of homemade bread, marmalade, cold meat and cheese, apple dumplings or her famous cinnamon rice pudding properly packed in a picnic basket— these must have had a powerful impact on young Will.

Indeed, these courtship excursions would lay the foundation for what would eventually provide the means of awakening Will's interior vocation. Indeed, throughout his life a long walk in the country would remain his deepest and most satisfying form of recreation. It was a pleasure inspired by Will's love for Hannah and her fidelity to the past. It was a courtship pleasure that helped to heal a deep wound in the lives of each. It also paved the way for the eventual emergence of essential, or personal, vocation.

The countryside and football fields of Oldbury Parish would undergo a transformation in the eyes of Hannah and Will. He would learn to look upon a meadow and perceive the pastoral presence that can be found in nature's beauty. Through Will's participation in organized sport, she would learn that the joy of victory and the heartache of loss can both be humbly accepted, endured, and openly shared. Through these ordinary activities each was being healed of the past and formed in the discipline of simplicity.

In his old age, Will enjoyed drinking tea from a saucer, but you can imagine the awkwardness he must have experienced in the tea rooms of the parish villages. I am confident he would have gone, wanting desperately to please his young Hannah. When football was in season, she would have returned the affection by attending every match, readily sharing him with his mates and fans. Victory on the field was generally followed by boisterous rounds of ale and sausage at the nearest public house. If the behavior of her final years provides a clue, win or lose, she would have thoroughly enjoyed every outing. If it meant sharing her handsome Will with his chums and adoring fans, so be it! Win or lose, she would put forth the effort to make the occasion a celebration.

Our formation in the art of relating requires effort. However, it is not an effort put forth by the self of pride. Rather, the effort to relate must spring from the humble, liberated self of faith, a self realized through the experience of play.

In Will's company Hannah did indeed develop the freedom to have fun. In the process of being courted, she seems to have learned all of the pub songs. Some of the rather bawdy songs of the music halls also found their way into her repertoire as well. Later in life, she would be called upon to entertain at family gatherings with such songs as "Pussycat's Ball" (otherwise known as the "Chimneysweep's Song"), until one of the more proper family members would gasp: "Mother!" Hannah would stop, but the song would instantly be replaced by her irrepressible giggle.

In her imagination her "gentleman" father may have set the standard of propriety. Phoebe, her mother, may have taught the value of patience and hard work. Will, however, had a distinct hand in adding another dimension to Hannah's life. He taught her the value of play and the freedom for having "a rousing good time." In her adult life the wheeze and snort of her laughter was a statement with which she would honor the dictates of propriety but, thanks to Will's quiet, passionate influence, she would "'ave a good load of fun doin' the job too!" Through Will's intercession in her life, her natural gregariousness found adoration, affirmation, and support. She also discovered that formation in the art of relating simply does not happen on its own. It requires the persistence and encouragement of people who care.

During courtship, however, Will challenged Hannah to do more than just have fun. Indeed, this was already a disposition underway before they met; it was part of his attraction. He did, though, enable her to deepen her sense of play and move forward, beyond the painful past. Indeed, each challenged and invited the other to accept the past and allow the horizon of hope to inform, guide, and direct the present. Neither would allow the other to face the harsh moments of life fortified only with pride. Through the challenge and mystery of first encounter, each would have a profound and reciprocal impact on the other: Will's gave birth to the value of quiet—Hannah's gave birth to the value of fun.

Through and with each other, their personal and relational life would develop to the full not by way of material accomplishment, but by way of perception. Each would help the other to develop *awareness;* awareness at the *wonder* and *mystery* of existence. Wonder would transform their sense of personal pain into a suffering of spirit and of soul; it would enable each to become empowered by hope. They would grow beyond the idealized and false promises of courtship and learn to challenge each other not to face the harsh blows of life with an infatuated self-determination to reverse the process.

In so doing, each enabled the other to avoid the entrapment of affliction. They entered courtship fortified with wonder, but their sense of hope would persist while each underwent detachment from the fantasies of perfection inspired by youthful illusion. In the process of stripping illusion, the power of hope would facilitate a more personal and flexible connection to life. Courtship would prepare the way for personal emergence. The pain and suffering of the past would be admitted into their relationship, but only as a messenger that suffering is not an end in itself and therefore something to be reversed. Hannah would learn to stop expecting Will to be perfect; he would do the same for her. Each would learn to bear witness to the value of vulnerability and thus provide deeper access to the world of intimacy we all desire. Each would learn that when we see each other as perfect, the self of vulnerability is denied access to our circle of relating.

Every loving encounter is played out against a background of brokenness; this is the ascetic that life's potential harshness holds for people of faith. Relationships inevitably are broken and new ones are formed out of a mix of pain and desire. When we view the life each lived before they met, we discover that neither Hannah nor Will was exempt from the ascetic process of intimacy. The formation story of their public and interior vocations was underway long before either knew of the other. Their marriage was not made in heaven; it was formed out of an anxious, loving search to find the *perfect one*, the one who would heal the brokenness of the past.

Espousal is a term for spiritual marriage; buried deep within its root is the notion of promise.[14] Romantics that we are, we tend to hear the wedding music as a love song for the future. However, in *The Dark Night* and *The Spiritual Canticle*, John of the Cross pointedly reminds us to consider the darkness from which our longings spring.[15] Our history of pain is visible in the awkwardness of first encounter. It is as if our integrity is reminding us that in the presence of another we must be aware of our inherent vulnerability. Sr. Rose Clarisse Gadoury formulates the difficulty: "The awkwardness of first encounter is not so much where we are going, but where each of us has been!"[16]

Marriage: A Wedding of Broken Relationships

In 1903, while Phoebe and Hannah were still keeping their Union Street vigil, waiting in vain for Thomas to return, Will was growing toward adulthood among the industry and playing fields of Langly. "Hard work, hard play, education is frivolous"—this was the philosophy of life in the home of "John the Bruiser." Will submitted to his father's injunctions. The elder Mister Greaves seems to have been unaware that his harsh approach might be providing the impetus for the escapist adventure some of his children, Will included, were contemplating. Following the example of his sister Hannah, Will emigrated to America. At eighteen, he had the physical maturity to work with adults. Yet, he was also possessed of youthful exuberance and could enjoy the thrill of an adventure.

Will was one of a legion of young men determined to make their mark in America. He was drawn by the energy and power of a land which, like him, was emerging from adolescence into adulthood. He was well prepared by the philosophy and discipline of John Greaves's house. The American Dream would easily become his personal dream, he thought. In rapid succession, he found lodging, a job, and a football club. His week was devoted to working in the foundry, saving money, and riding his bicycle to his old game with the new name: soccer.

Will's life would continue in this vein for three years, but in 1906 he would learn that the patient, quiet, Amplias Smith Greaves had suddenly died. Will was stunned, totally unprepared for the event. She was so strong, so young. In sadness and shock, his dream would be dispossessed by concern for his family. Chastened by this blow, he returned to England. He had no way of knowing his heart was being prepared for yet another event. On his return there, he attempted to resume his old way of living but could not do so, for the relationship taken from him by death had formed a permanent hole in his life. The playing field enabled him to take distance from his suffering. It would also bring him the attention of Hannah Bently Browning.

While Will was attempting to cope with the loneliness created by his mother's death, in another part of town a lonely child was keeping vigil for her father and emerging into young adulthood. By the time they would finally meet, life would have conspired to lead each, separately, through the dark night of a broken relationship. The ascetics of everyday life had provided an opportunity for dispossession and detachment, confronting each with the essential vulnerability of being human. As a woman of faith, Hannah had an intuitive sense that God, as parent, shared empathically in such moments of awareness. Early in life, she had learned that loss by death or separation shatters any illusion of permanence and power. In learning to be patiently open in such moments, complaisance and the dynamic of pride would begin to lose the power to direct her life.

When they would finally meet, the loss of her father, felt since childhood, would make her keenly aware of Will's pain. She would also know the blinding speed with which the darkness of loss can occur. She would know the urgent longing and anxious searching for that perfect other that death can precipitate. She too had searched the faces of strangers looking for her future and her past. When she and Will finally met, she could recognize the look on Will's face. In her marriage, she would grow continually toward a deeper understanding of that look she had found.

In their first encounter, Will would share a similar experience. He would gaze upon her face in wonder, looking upon her from within his pain. He would see her vulnerability and the promise of *espousal*. The lonely, hungry look we see on the face of those we love is a promise that seems to offer relief from the agonies of life. Although he could not understand the significance of what he saw, through Hannah's care he would learn. She, in turn, would benefit as well. Each would move toward responding to the promise of espousal, perceived in those courtship moments when each saw the other's vulnerability.

The promise and gift of courtship's first encounter would gradually be deepened over the next six and a half decades of their life. The vowed relationship they would form on that December 25 would be formed against a background of broken relationships, but it would also give birth to a disciplined and loving awareness, one that would promote a deeper, wider, more transcendent sense of hope than the memories of the past.

Espousal: A Promise to Stare in the Darkness

Through the mystery and challenge of encounter, Hannah and Will would each be able to realize a new perspective. He would be able to look upon a meadow and see its quiet beauty. She would learn the value of silence and how to join the crowd in song. Together they would learn to face the darkness into which we are all inevitably and unceremoniously plunged by life's harshness. Through the mystery and challenge of encounter, each would learn that in brokenness, life opens a window of vulnerability through which the spirit of espousal encourages us to look. Throughout their life, each would encourage the other not to avert their gaze. She would be encouraged by religion. He would hear the invitation first in songs of victory and defeat, then whispered to him softly in the Pines. Through divergent experiences, each would learn to travel through circles of intimacy accented by joy or tragedy. They would learn to act, or wait, together.

Unlike Fitzgerald and Zelda or Vladimir and Estragon, Hannah and Will would develop a different kind of dependence. Their dependence would not be based upon determination or despair, but upon wonder and awe at the mystery of life's adventure. At the beginning of their relationship they would look at each other through the eyes of need. But by their middle age, each would learn to see the other as an individual who could respond to the invitation to care. In their mutual commitment, they would face life's blows by learning how to bend, each depending on the other for challenge and support. Each would assist the other not to get caught by the pride that seeks to reverse the process of growth inherent in those blows.

When Hannah and Will first met, each perceived the invitation of infatuation to become a witness for the other. They grew in the ability to be aware and to respond. The awkwardness and wonder of first encounter would enable mind, heart, and memory to be healed. The perspective of each, narrowed by the pain of broken relationships, would be reopened to incorporate the challenging, healing vision of another. They would get beyond the awkwardness of first encounter and learn to see and learn to care.

Eventually, they would learn to laugh in the face of life's setbacks. They would not laugh *at* life's harshness, but with flexibility would confront and accept the pain and not attempt to dominate or reverse the process. Each would learn the wisdom of suffering: that life's painful moments open windows of vulnerability. They found that their task was to keep the windows open long enough not to be overwhelmed by the impermanence they saw. They would learn the secret and promise of intimacy: to weep at brokenness and to wait and stand in hope for new circles of wholeness to emerge. They learned to heal-in-care and hope-in-wonder. Through this, they would grow in humility and faith. They not only kept their sense of humor; it was a sign of their detachment.

Teresa of Avila defines humility as standing in the truth of our existence.[17] Adrian van Kaam tells us that humility and humor are associated by their shared Latin root: *humus*, meaning soil or ground.[18] Experientially, he notes, humor and humility share more than a common origin; they are the dispositions, the attitudinal tools needed to cope with pride.

Together Hannah and Will learned to respect the mystery of suffering and to see within their pain the promise of renewal. With faith inspired by the promise of espousal, they took their marriage vows and humbly learned to laugh not only in each other's presence, but in the presence of their God as well. The echo of their laughter continues to be heard in the formation stories of sadness and joy told by family, neighbor, and friend.

The reality of their witness continues to be visible. It is seen whenever the people they touched are open to life's pain and suffering and make the surprising discovery that they are not broken but transformed.

Obedience is the joining of the links of the eternal round. Obedience is the other side of the creative will. . . . If we do the will of God eternal life is ours—no mere continuity of existence, for that in itself is worthless as hell, but a being that is one with the essential life.

—George MacDonald, *Unspoken Sermons*

Love is a circle that doth restless move
in the same sweet eternity of love.

—Robert Herrick, "Love What It Is"

Intimate Circles

What is intimacy? In the context of Hannah and Will's relationship, it was an experience lived on different levels during three separate phases of their relational life. During young adulthood they underwent a *courtship phase* in which they shared an *intimacy of the senses*. Within this phase they learned to cope with the dark and lonely moments of their past. They also had to come to grips with their romantic dreams and feelings and the expectations that burst upon their lives with such insistence and urgency. Next, they negotiated the *middle-adulthood phase* during which they shared an *intimacy of friendship*. During this period they were able to relate to each other as individuals with personal integrity. As friends they learned to encounter each other with acceptance, tolerance, and understanding. Finally, somewhere in late adulthood, they entered a *mature phase* of relating. During this third and final phase they were able to move into a deeper relational circle, where an *intimacy of love* was evoked. During this final phase of their relational life, they could be present to each other in a manner that was playful, tender, and deeply personal. The love they revealed to each other was also shared with others in the form of care.

We are cautioned by van Kaam: "The intimacy of friendship does not necessarily unfold into the deeper relational intimacy of love"; for Hannah and Will it did.[1] Indeed, their relationship offers clear instruction on the gradual formation of mature, personal presence found in *authentic* intimacy. The unfolding of their relational life reveals an ability to move in two distinctly different relational directions: *horizontally* and *vertically*. As they moved along the horizon of daily life, they experienced the distance and closeness that is necessary for the experience of intimacy. But the way they encountered suffering enabled each to ascend higher and go deeper into the intimacy adventure.

Intimacy: A Movement in Two Directions

The horizontal movement of intimacy is visible in our personal, daily interactions with each other; here, van Kaam's caution is correct, the intimacy of love may not be found. What does exist, however, is recognizable as something that satisfies the yearning and alleviates the frustration of a certain kind of loneliness, one that flows from a desire for or-

dinary intimacy. This can occur in a variety of relational set-
tings; it can unfold between old friends, new acquaintances,
or among strangers. The following captures the essential features of this particular kind of intimacy:

> [It unfolds in experiences] of being with and for others
> in which we discard the label or mask of exterior iden-
> tity, revealing ourselves as persons who are vulnerable;
> [or in] experiences of being present such that we feel
> understood, accepted and known. [During such mo-
> ments] there is the warmth of [emotional or physical]
> nearness but we also retain the freedom to be separate.
> [Such experiences] involve disclosure with its ac-
> companying words, signs, and gestures, and they can
> occur in moments where words are unnecessary.
> [Generally such experiences occur in a pleasant event,
> but can be initiated in harshness.][2]

Such moments of ordinary intimacy can satisfy the yearning and alleviate the frustration of a certain kind of loneliness, but they also can incorporate all that it means to be
alone. Ordinarily, such experiences occur in the presence of
others. Such intimate moments also occur in a variety of set-
tings: a moonlit walk along the beach, at a picnic in the country, or in a group gathered "'round the Christmas pudding."
It may be argued that place is, or is not, essential. It is clear,
though, that intimacy in everyday life provides an atmosphere where a variety of experiences such as understanding, acceptance, consolation, or reconciliation may
occur. On this level, intimacy may be characterized as re-
demptive, healing, or in some way significantly transformative for the variety of relationships that may exist. The
intimacy of everyday life may be seen as historically pivotal,
where a bond is established or deepened, a commitment

made or re-awakened, when an important realization or awareness occurs or is remembered.[3] Care, in the Heideggerian sense of interest, concern, and solicitude, facilitates the movement on this dimension.[4]

Clearly, this was at work in Hannah and Will's relationship. Each took time to be aware. They would pause in their daily routine to notice the other and if they thought it was warranted, would not hesitate to inquire about the well-being of the other. Throughout their relational life, but during the third phase in particular, they practiced a personal discipline that enabled them to relate. By the time they entered maturity they were skilled in the art of ordinary intimacy. Their skill was noticed and enjoyed by others.

Intimacy also moves in a *vertical*, transcendent dimension. Thomas Merton speaks to this dimension when he writes of our need to respond to the invitation to be drawn to our deepest, truest center. In this center, he instructs, we are made ready for a different kind of participation with others. At this center, we encounter the self of "perfect charity" that asks nothing more, or less, than our willingness to say yes and become our "true self."[5]

This "self" is the self of interior, "essential," or personal vocation addressed by Simone Weil.[6] It is a self dispossessed of any counterfeit or illusory self. It is, Merton tells us, our most unique, authentic, and "true" self.[7] It is the person we become, having encountered and said yes to love's effort. It is a self liberated from the determined and inflexible dictates of pride. This true self is formed by the attitude with which we encounter everyday suffering and pain, an attitude that is being formed throughout life.

If Hannah and Will's relationship offers any instruction, it teaches us that when we undergo the horizontal movement through the phases of everyday relational intimacy, we embark on a quest that cannot be satisfied if we persist only in that direction. We must be prepared to embark on a vertical, transcendent journey as well. The pursuit of this journey, though, is not for the faint-hearted. Throughout history, writers such as Paul, Augustine, Ignatius, John of the Cross, and Teresa of Avila have warned us of the perils, diminution, darkness, absurdity, desolation, and pain we will encounter. Through their work we are put on notice that the journey of transcendence requires an openness to suffering.

Unfortunately, out of the body of literature warning us of the danger, we have developed a spiritual hero worship which, in our culture, has led us to overlook the suffering and transformation of ordinary people such as Hannah and Will. Thus, we are left with the belief that only a handful of the greatest saints have negotiated this spiritual minefield we encounter on the transcendent journey of *relational intimacy*.

Perhaps it is fortunate that Hannah and Will never conceptualized their journey as spiritual; for in the most ordinary and unself-conscious way they invited each other to play, laugh, and sometimes repair their relationship. But something else was at work in their life, something that lent support to their commitment, enabling them to confront and challenge the illusions, distortions, and disappointments encountered during life's tougher moments. In the process of relating, they underwent considerable suffering, but through mutual witness could gain access to a higher and deeper level of simplicity and gentleness. Each emerged as *person*: separate, unique, and capable of transforming ordinary intimacy into a creative personal experience that enabled each to withstand and grow beyond their deeply painful experiences of the past and their expectations of the future.

Vows: Initiating an Intimate Ascent

On the horizontal dimension of daily living, Hannah and Will passed through separate phases of relational intimacy,

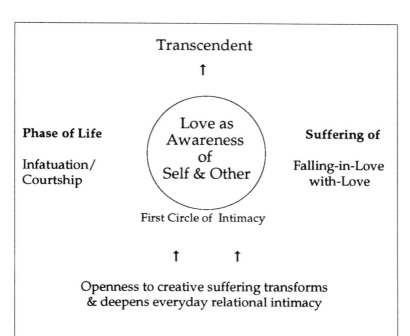

Transcendent

↑

Phase of Life   Love as   **Suffering of**
                          Awareness
Infatuation/   of   Falling-in-Love
Courtship   Self & Other   with-Love

First Circle of Intimacy

↑   ↑

Openness to creative suffering transforms
& deepens everyday relational intimacy

As we travel across the horizon of everyday relational intimacy from cradle to grave, it is inevitable we will encounter pain and suffering. During adolescence and young adulthood, many of the harsh moments we experience are promoted by our blindness to self and the distortion of others. The first significantly transformative moment on the relational journey occurs during the phase of infatuation/courtship when we develop a more informed awareness of self and a tolerance of others.

Figure 4—Dynamics of Intimacy

from distance to closeness, from acquaintances to friends. They struggled with the experiences, values, myths, dreams, and expectations that can either liberate or inhibit intimacy, deepen it or keep it shallow.

Hannah and Will stood side by side at their wedding and gave testimony to their willingness to struggle with the perils and rewards we encounter if we are willing to embark on the adventurous journey of intimacy:

> . . . for better or for worse;
> for richer or for poorer;
> in sickness and in health;
> until death us do part. . . .

In the solemn utterance of these words before minister and congregation, they proclaimed their intent to establish a covenant with self, other, *and* God. They declared fidelity when they would meet the bright side: "better," "richer," "health." They also proclaimed a willingness to persist when struck by the darker side as well: "poverty," "sickness," "death."

Through a mutual declaration of intention, Hannah and Will embarked upon a journey in two directions. They had some idea of the horizontal, but little understanding that on the vertical, three different adventures would unfold. In the *courtship* of daily life, each would encounter and respond to the intimacy of *invitation,* where they would meet each other, fall in love, and get to know each other as lover, spouse, parent, and struggle with issues of the flesh. In the *mid-life* phase they would encounter each other through an intimacy of *transformation,* where fidelity to the public vows they exchanged would facilitate discovery of "essential," or personal, vocation. This enabled them to be and act as friends.

Finally, when each became mature, they entered the phase of *espousal*, where they would participate in an intimacy of *personal witness*. In this adventure, the person each discovered would facilitate the expression of a constant, thoughtful love that was simple, humble, and generous, while also being prudent and discrete.

In this third, or maturity, phase, each in a very separate and unique way would learn the final lesson of detachment, a lesson readily shared with others. In this phase, their witness went beyond the social imperative of maintaining appearances. During the days of Will's wake, many of his old friends were as surprised as I when Hannah commented on his eccentricities. She could be prudent, but even during the most grueling of life's painful moments, she would not pretend, and neither would Will.

Through the third phase of the vertical journey, fidelity to the covenant they made enabled each to become a truthful witness to the bright and dark moments of daily existence. As a consequence, their journey through the vertical intertwined with the "reality" of the horizontal; the lessons learned lent a dimension of depth and meaning to daily life, enabling each to meet its harsh blows with a self more flexible and grounded than the self of pride. Together they developed the realization that suffering only ends in despair when we believe it must be dominated and reversed.

Hannah and Will grew to understand that relating on the horizon of daily life featured competitive values that accentuate pride. Fidelity to the covenant they established added another dimension to their life: the freedom to formulate other choices based on alternative values. Vladimir, Estragon, and young Fitzgerald were constrained by pride. Through fidelity to the fundamental meaning of their vows, Hannah and Will could develop an alternative perspective to the suffering of life; the alternative enabled each to realize that the dark, harsh moments of life can co-exist alongside the more agreeable. The *vertical* gave them freedom to be flexible while they moved across the horizon of everyday relating.

The First Vertical Circle: Intimacy as Awareness

Hannah and Will's struggle to integrate the ordinary and transcendent dimensions of intimacy enabled them to eventually celebrate a liturgy of relationship where each was both celebrant and witness. The harshness they had faced in daily life had worn away the false, revealing something genuine in each. After Will died, we understood that they had realized an awareness and acceptance that was a living, charitable, and liberating tolerance. When we described them as "close," we were really describing them as *knowing* each other, we were pointing to their ability to participate in an experience of intimate adoration; not the dewy-eyed worship of adolescent infatuation, but an informed reverence: a *staring in kindness.*

They could look at each other and behold both gift and limitation, without resorting to the pretense of illusions. They could practice their faith in each other through acts of care that were tolerant, appreciative, and loving, acts that affirmed and liberated each other. They spent time with each other, nourishing their commitment, but each was free to be alone. In allowing the other to be alone, each could discover the deeper self of longing and of limit contained within infatuation; each was able to discover that we need others to facilitate the discovery of who and what we are.

The friendship Hannah and Will established at the end of their life would seem to contradict van Kaam's caution[8] (quoted earlier, on page 91). However, unlike the intimacy of most, theirs incorporated both dimensions of the intimate adventure. The depth of care they realized for each other was readily shared with others without interfering with the commitment each had made. The quality of their relationship in the third phase of their journey suggests that the lesson of friendship was incorporated and transformed. Friends are able to see, overlook, and at times challenge each other's flaws; lovers are not, because the urgency of their need for perfection makes them unable to tell the other what is wrong. Hannah and Will generally knew when it was appropriate to speak; sometimes they erred and there was bedlam. Eventually, their sense of humor would rectify the situation. They had moved beyond romance; they had grown to be something more than friends. Their relationship had matured into a compassionate and tolerant reverence that could only be called love.

Years of struggle had given birth to a wisdom that rendered their friendship authentic. The course of travel across the horizon of daily life taught them the need for tolerance, but it also exposed them to the self of pride. Travel through the vertical was made possible by a mutual commitment strengthened by faith; it disposed their friendship toward love. Each discovered the secret lesson of the vertical: When we move *against* the other, we abandon hope. Fortified with wisdom, each could return to the plane of everyday life, defenses could be lowered, the illusions wrought by infatuated pride would disappear, and they could look upon each other with eyes of tolerance and awareness.

The Second Vertical Circle: Intimacy as Integrity

In the first intimate circle, Hannah and Will learned they were each called to fall-in-love; this was the beginning of their journey toward love as *awareness*. Here, they wrestled with the issue of acceptability. They also learned the inspiring and devastating effect a dream of perfection can have upon those we profess to love. Once we fall-in-love-with-love, we must next learn how to love each other.

In the second circle, Hannah and Will learned to hear and speak the lesson of *integrity*. When called upon to address the

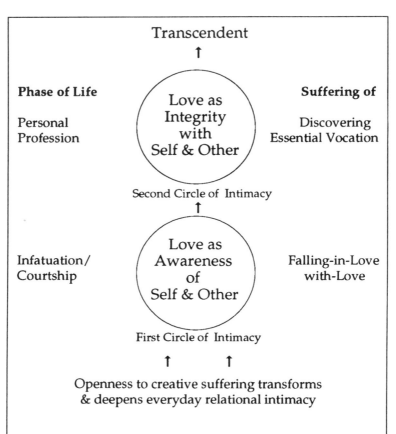

Transcendent
↑

Phase of Life

Personal
Profession

Love as
Integrity
with
Self & Other

Suffering of

Discovering
Essential Vocation

Second Circle of Intimacy
↑

Infatuation/
Courtship

Love as
Awareness
of
Self & Other

Falling-in-Love
with-Love

First Circle of Intimacy

↑   ↑

Openness to creative suffering transforms
& deepens everyday relational intimacy

On our journey to find a loving response from others, we encounter many obstacles, not the least of which is the refusal to accept ourselves for who and what we are before both self and other. The lessons of tolerance and self-acceptance develop during the phase of life when we allow ourselves to enter the aloneness of creative suffering and discover our true self. We emerge from the experience of solitude in touch with our integrity and dispossessed of the need to make others submit to our urgent longing to be loved.

Figure 5—Dynamics of Intimacy

issue of acceptability, each would honestly tell the other, "Sometimes you are—sometimes you are not!" Toward the end of their journey through the first vertical circle, some time in the middle-adulthood years, the need to maintain an illusion of perfection was losing its claim on their attention. Their awareness of each other was becoming more and more inspired by that freedom of tolerance and acceptance that underlies forgiveness. In their search for intimacy, they had suffered too much to try to maintain the hard shallowness of a false reality. On their journey through the middle years, the self of pride was softened by a sense of wonder and of awe; this enabled each to see with less distortion. Within the womb of that second circle, each gave birth to something that brought life into their everyday relational world. Their relationship began to assume a depth that moved beyond ordinary friendship, transforming each into a friend with integrity. The emergence of integrity was fostered by the intimate moments we call acceptance, understanding, support, affirmation, etc., all of which are readily available on the horizon of relationship when we put forth the effort to care.

When Will died, Hannah became very lonely. We have already observed how each had learned to be alone. However, by the middle of their lives each was learning *detachment*. In the second phase of relational life, we apply the lessons of the first: We learn to accept each other as we are. Slowly, Hannah and Will learned, in care, to let the other be. If Will was feeling cantankerous and she was experiencing the desire to be close, she could challenge or accept. She had learned that if it were within his power to address her need he would try. She had learned the value of gentleness and patience. She had also learned that there exists a desire to be alone that must be both respected and supported. Will, too, had heard the lesson whispered softly in the Pines: ". . . we are alone together you and I, and we cannot make each other unalone. . . ."

Such was their intimacy. Within their relationship they could witness to the existence of a solitude where the deepest of our longings can be found.

In the second phase of their relational life, each had grown in awareness of the need of solitude, and in the ability to practice it. John Dunne writes of this as the emergence of wisdom. It is the recognition that I cannot make the other be God for me: "Self appears when I am alone. . . . the soul is dark until our hearts are free, until we are willing to walk alone, until our heart's longing has become consciously a longing for God."[9] Until that moment arrives, we cannot tolerate being alone, not to mention with each other.

Separately and perhaps at different times, each emerged from the second phase of the relational journey able to accept the yearning and frustration of loneliness. In this phase, each had learned that there is an irreducible loneliness, one not taken away even when we are very close to others.[10] Each had learned to be alone. In being alone the infatuated self of fascination that makes us cling was finally transformed. A more autonomous and tolerant self emerged, one that could celebrate both self and other. Unlike the self of infatuated pride, this new self could stand alone. This more personal self could undergo the aloneness necessary to hear the longing in the heart of the other. This new self could see with clarity the limited ability we possess when we attempt to respond to life's harsh blows fortified only with our pride. But this new, transformed self had the wisdom to seek support by letting others know what it desired.

The Third Vertical Circle: Intimacy as Presence

In the fourth century, hermits and cenobites by the hundreds went into the desert to witness their faith. Their legacy is a compendium of stories and sayings that call us to the awareness that human witness must always be an openness to the

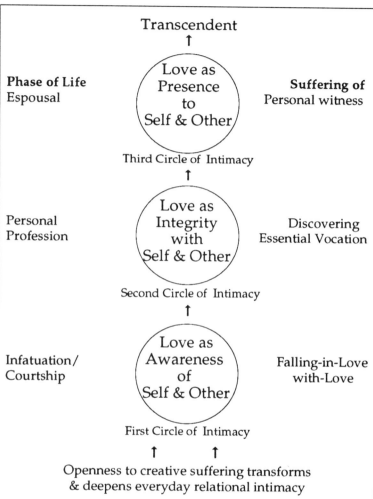

Transcendent
↑

Phase of Life		Suffering of
Espousal	Love as Presence to Self & Other	Personal witness

Third Circle of Intimacy
↑

Personal Profession	Love as Integrity with Self & Other	Discovering Essential Vocation

Second Circle of Intimacy
↑

Infatuation/ Courtship	Love as Awareness of Self & Other	Falling-in-Love with-Love

First Circle of Intimacy
↑   ↑

Openness to creative suffering transforms
& deepens everyday relational intimacy

In learning to be alone we become more self-accepting and tolerant of others; pride is tempered. The self of wisdom begins to emerge as we become both free and available to both self and other. In this phase of relational formation, we are more aware of our vulnerability to disappointment, but we are also more liberated in our ability to articulate our needs. During this phase of the relational journey, we also make the curious discovery that even our needs have been transformed.

Figure 6—Formation Dynamics of Intimacy

divine. These people of the desert remind us that we are to be forgetful when we think the reverence of others is intended just for us. Thomas Merton tells this story of humility, simplicity, and poverty:

> . . . Once a certain provincial judge came to see Abbot Simon and the elder took the belt he had on and went to the top of the date palm as though he were a workman picking dates. But they, approaching, asked him: "Where is the hermit who lives in this part of the desert?" To which he replied: "There is no hermit around here." At this they departed. On another occasion a different judge came to see him, and his companions, running on ahead of the judge, said: "Father, get ready. A judge who has heard about you is on his way out here to ask your blessing." The elder said: "You can be sure I will get ready." And covering himself with all his garments he took some bread and cheese and sat down in the entry to his cell and began to eat. The judge and all his retainers arrived and saw him eating and hailed him with contempt. "Is this the hermit monk we heard so much about?" they asked. They swung around immediately and headed back where they had come from. . . .[11]

On the horizon of daily relational existence, the adoring but expectant demand of others is often much more subtle. In daily life, it is rare for anyone to respond with the discipline, humility, and wisdom of Abbot Simon. For Hannah and Will, it took a lifetime of struggle before each could consistently enter the third vertical circle and form a relationship of faith where such humble witness is possible. When they did enter, their presence to others was considerably less dramatic than that of Abbot Simon. However, toward the end of their life together they did in fact learn to confront and tame the natural narcissism of the infatuated self of pride, a self that wants the other to adore our power, authority, skill, or wealth. The lessons Hannah and Will learned within the third phase of their relationship have relevance to help us meet the sinfulness of today. The witness of their final years demonstrates an attitude to combat the competitive distractions of a too busy life, which seemingly requires us to hurry, force our point of view upon the other, yell loudly, pull rank, or in myriad ways do violence to the gentle voice of truth dwelling within the frail existence of every human being.

Within the third vertical circle, Hannah and Will each learned the art of intimacy, which masters *dwelling, surrender,* and *allowing the other to be,* while still holding the other accountable. Within this circle, each learned to approach life with a new sense of purpose. Like Abbot Simon, they learned to turn away the false demands of others who were rushing to acquire the fruit of love's effort without undergoing the journey on their own. The wisdom they reflected might be put as follows:

Don't take yourself so seriously;
intimacy takes time and if
you are not humble, patient, and flexible,
when the harsh blows come
or when people make demands and tell you who you
    ought to be,
you will crack and sink into despair.

In the final two verses of Psalm 139 we are invited to *risk* and to *surrender.*[12] The intimacy that evolved in Hannah and Will's journey through the third circle provides clear instruction: In the course of everyday relating, there are moments when we must drop our defenses, expose our vulnerability, and tell the other what we want. When we listen through the ears of pride this will sound harsh, demanding. When we stand in the circle of *personal witness*, the words and meaning are transformed. We can listen and speak with the tenderness of St. Paul when he boasts he is the best of lovers!

Gradually, Hannah and Will could expose the self of vulnerability to each other with some consistency. She could tell him what she wanted; he could do the same for her. At their respective funerals, the long, long line of mourners was mute testimony to their journey into the third circle. Once we gain access to that circle, we are sent back into the world to be a gentle, loving witness. For in that circle we are reminded that our formation story is a long and constant struggle in learning how to be with others. And, we are taught, the lesson must be shared.

Hannah and Will's story is a love story. The final lesson of their journey speaks of passion, not the passion of a lover's pride that seeks to dominate, but a passion more like that of Jeremiah when he was sent to preach: "Ah, Lord Yahweh," speaks Jeremiah, "look, I do not know how to speak: I am a child. . . ."

In response to this simple act of faith, Yahweh tenderly put a hand on Jeremiah's mouth and the words were given.[13] Jeremiah became as a child and he was able to enter the circle of personal witness. Rahner refers to this attitude as "mature childhood";[14] it is, simultaneously, the most simple and profound expression of our relational existence as transcendent. It is an essential disposition formed within the third circle. There, intimacy becomes an attitude that gives birth to a quality of presence promoted by simplicity. Richard Foster writes:

. . . simplicity of heart can only flourish in the fertile soil of trust, and it is the Old Testament's revelation of the faithfulness and goodness of God that opens the door to that trust.[15]

Hannah and Will were humble, simple people who learned to trust in the manner of Jeremiah. Their sense of trust had evolved out of a lifetime of working at their relationship. The effort to be faithful to their vows had forced them to confront the primary obstacles to intimacy. They faced the determined obstinateness promoted by natural narcissism, which makes us unwilling to settle for who and what we are; they faced the pride we carry in our hearts that forces us to resist being available to self and other; they faced the hidden fantasies promoted by our dreams that seduce us into the belief that we are responsible for our own formation; finally, they faced the greatest obstacle of all, the narcissistic pride that inhibits obedience to the call to be intimate.

In their old age, Hannah and Will had been "worn to the nub" by the work required for human intimacy. Their bodies had grown tired, bent by the burden of relating. Simone Weil writes:

> . . . if we are worn out it means that we are becoming submissive to time as matter is; thought is forced to pass from one instant to the next without laying hold of the past or future: *this is what it means to obey. . . .*[16]

Each had been worn down, but not worn out, for they had grown skilled in the art and wisdom of bringing life's creative energy to others. They had learned to be obedient to that voice within that speaks the hidden request of intimacy: "Am I of value?" They had learned to be obedient to the instruction given in the third circle: "Open your eyes and see!" They could look at others and in the peacefulness of their expression would reveal: "No, you are not perfect, nor is that necessary. Your only requirement in life is to simply learn to be yourself with all your gifts and limits."

Toward the end of their journey, they, like Abbot Simon, had grown weary of those intent on promoting distraction. They were content to look at each other, and in so doing they could find what they were searching for. Each could look and see that their value was to be found upon the other's face. They had finally confronted the greatest obstacle of all; each could look and see the other. They could maintain contact with each other and discover the joy of existence found within the frailty of our wounded nature. Toward the end, they had learned to be submissive. Within the third circle, they would hear the final lesson: that while we search for heart's desire upon the face of strangers, *heart's desire is found upon the face of those for whom we care.*

Hannah and Will were simple, ordinary, poor people. What little they owned they were willing to share with family, friend, and neighbor. Several months after Hannah died, her family began the final, sad task of dispersing their belongings. Aside from the few furnishings they owned, their personal effects, mostly gifts from others, barely covered the dining room table. "Not much, Tom," Elsie said, and as we looked we began to tell each other stories we remembered about their humility, generosity, and sense of being playful.

Now, more than a decade and a half later, I see that their legacy went far beyond material goods. Theirs was a legacy of awareness that love is an effort *and* an outcome. They did not own material goods, but they readily shared what they had discovered on both the everyday and transcendent dimensions of the intimate adventure. Their legacy is the lesson that if we are willing to expend the effort to love, we will experience pain, but we will also experience the joy and rapture of the experience of being alive. Their legacy is the inspiration that in order to understand what it means to be intimate, we simply must persist in the effort.

The reminiscences I shared that sad day with Elsie have served as a reminder. Hannah and Will were persistent; separately and together they "'ad a good load of fun doin' the job too!" But all who came in contact with them were invited to share in the celebration. This is the sacral secret that lies at the heart of the relational experience we call *intimacy*.

In their struggle to meet on the horizon of relationship, Hannah and Will took vows that established a covenant; from that point forward they began to ascend a secret ladder. Fidelity to their covenant enabled them to persist through three distinct phases on the spiritual journey of relational life. Their adventure took them from the romantic illusions of courtship to the loving awareness of maturity; during each phase they met pain and suffering. And during each of these moments on the journey they were faithful not only to each other, but to the essence of their vows. Their mutual commitment eventually brought them to a place of adoration where they found a privacy, peace, and joy they willingly shared with others. To understand and practice the attitude that fostered the union they found, we need only follow Richard Foster's advice[17] and turn to the book of Wisdom (18:14–15):

> . . . when peaceful silence lay over all
> and night had run the half of her swift course,
> down from the heavens, from the royal throne,
> leaped your all-powerful word. . . .

Perhaps the sacral secret at the heart of intimacy is revealed to us when we, like Hannah and Will, become a people of obedience and assume a posture of humility before the throne. When I look at Hannah and Will's life, their lesson seems to be that when we lower our heads, our hearts will begin to swell with an inner fullness that will eventually burst apart with laughter. Thus begins the adventure of intimacy. Humility, practiced in integrity and persistence, initiates the relational equivalent of the "big bang."[18] Humility, practiced in solitude and play, sets in motion creative forces that form a universe of relational possibilities that incorporate and transform life's harsh blows.

In our family, the echo of their intimate laughter continues to be heard whenever the Christmas pudding is set afire. In this simple act, a new world of intimacy is created once again. Its originating source? The gentle and all-powerful word Hannah and Will heard as *care*.[19]

Notes

Preface

1. George MacDonald, *Creation in Christ* (Wheaton, Ill.: Harold Shaw Publishers, 1976), p. 191, edited by Rolland Hein (from the original publication, *Unspoken Sermons*, vol. II, "The Creation of Sons," sermon 18 subtitled "Life," 1885).

Introduction

1. St. John of the Cross, *The Collected Works of St. John of the Cross*, trans. by Kieran Kavanaugh and Otilio Rodriguez (Washington, D.C.: Institute of Carmelite Studies Publications, 1979), p. 59 (Prologue of the Ascent, 7-8). (Note: All remaining references in this text are taken from the 1991 edition.)

2. The group consisted of religious and secular professionals under the direction of Sister Mary Rose Clarisse Gadoury, S.S.A., D.Min. Other members of the group were Rev. Raymond Bertrand, S.J. (deceased), Brother John Collins, C.F.X., Sister Mary Claire Allaire, S.S.A., Brother John Hamilton, C.F.X., Sister Mary Jeannette Robichaud, S.S.A., Carol J. Tyrrell, and myself. I continue to be indebted to their insight and scholarship.

3. Simone Weil, *Waiting for God* (New York: Harper & Row, 1973), trans. by Emma Crawford, pp. 43-57 (esp. p. 48).

4. A number of writers in the area of psychology and spirituality can be cited here. A representative sample are: Daniel Levinson, Adrian van Kaam, Evelyn Whitehead, and James Whitehead, whose works are cited throughout this text. The reader may also wish to consult James Fowler, and the religious work of Dennis Linn, Matthew Linn, and Sheila Fabricant, particularly *Healing the Eight Stages of Life* (New York: Paulist Press, 1988) and Benedict Groeschel, *Spiritual Passages* (New York: Crossroad, 1986).

Chapter 1—The Adventure of Intimacy

Opening Quote: Annie Dillard, *Holy the Firm* (New York: Bantam Books, 1979), pp. 42, 43.

1. Daniel Levinson, *The Seasons of a Man's Life* (New York: Ballantine, 1979). Levinson also addresses this issue in his work, "The Life Structure Development of Women in Early Adulthood," unpublished lecture, Yale University, November 1988. See especially p. 6 where he addresses the issue of relationship.

2. Thomas Tyrrell, *Urgent Longings* (Mystic, Conn.: Twenty-Third Publications, 1994), rev. ed.

3. Adrian van Kaam, *Formation of the Human Heart* (New York: Crossroad, 1986).

4. Daniel Levinson (*The Seasons of a Man's Life* and "The Life Structure Development of Women in Early Adulthood") makes this point, suggesting that these formative dreams are created by a multiplicity of forces outside the individual.

5. Daniel Levinson, *The Seasons of a Man's Life*.

6. Thomas Merton, "The Ascetic Life, Experience of God and Freedom," transcribed tape-recorded conference to novices by Robert McGregor, Mount St. Bernard; printed by trustees of the Merton Legacy Trust, 1974, pp. 64, 65. See also James Finley, *Merton's Palace of Nowhere* (Notre Dame, Ind.: Ave Maria Press, 1978) for an overview of Merton's use of the construct "true" and "false" self.

7. The settlement made provision for daily living expenses by providing access to the collection of rents from certain family holdings. Additionally, property and furnishings were transferred to provide a domicile for young Thomas and Phoebe and a fixed sum was put in trust to insure financial security.

8. T.S. Eliot, *Four Quartets* (New York: Harcourt Brace Jovanovich, 1971), pp. 13-20.

9. Thomas Merton, "Asceticism, Freedom and Experience of God," pp. 64, 65.

10. Thomas Merton, *New Seeds of Contemplation* (Gethsemani, Ky.: New Directions, 1961).

11. Bernard Boelen, *Personal Maturity: The Existential Dimension* (New York: Seabury Press, 1978), pp. 14-17.

12. Thomas Merton, *The Ascent to Truth* (New York: Harcourt Brace Jovanovich, 1981).

13. As translated by John Dunne, *Reasons of the Heart* (New York: Macmillan, 1978), p. 48.

14. Delmore Schwartz, *In Dreams Begin Responsibilities and Other Stories* (New York: New Directions, 1978).

Chapter 2—A Journey Across the Horizon of Relationship

Opening Quotes: T.S. Eliot, *Four Quartets* (New York: Harcourt Brace Jovanovich, 1971), from the poem "Burnt Norton," p. 15. C.S. Lewis, *Poems* (New York: Harcourt Brace Jovanovich, 1977), pp. 114-115.

1. Adrian van Kaam, *The Emergent Self* (Wilkes-Barre, Penn.: Dimension Press, 1968). See Book IV, "The Self and Reality," pp. 19-27. Thomas Merton, *New Seeds of Contemplation*, see pp. 233-238. St. Augustine, *Confessions* (Garden City, N.Y.: Doubleday, 1960), trans. by John Ryan.

2. St. John of the Cross, *The Ascent of Mount Carmel* (Washington, D.C.: I.C.S. Publications, 1991), trans. by Kieran Kavanaugh and Otilio Rodriguez, pp. 295-389. (Hereafter referred to as *Collected Works*). St. John of the Cross, *Collected Works, ibid.* See esp. pp. 353-457.

3. Judith Viorst, *Necessary Losses* (New York: Fawcett Gold Medal, 1993).

4. Harriet Goldhor Lerner, *The Dance of Intimacy* (New York: Harper & Row, 1989).

5. Their first son was named for Will; the second was named Thomas. At Joan's birth Hannah intended to honor her mother, but was voted down!

6. See Edith Hamilton, *Mythology* (New York: Mentor, 1942), pp. 87-88.

7. Isaiah 41:8–16.

8. St. John of the Cross, *Collected Works*, pp. 353-457.

9. José Ortega Y Gasset, *On Love: Aspects of a Single Theme* (New York: Meridian Books, World Publishing Co., 1966), p. 126.

10. Meister Eckhart, ed. by Franz Pfieffer, trans. by C. de B. Evans (London: John M. Watkins, 1947), p. 59 (from the sermon "*Scio hominem in Christo*") interpreted and translated by John Dunne, *The Reasons of the Heart*, p. 48: "When God laughs to the soul and the soul laughs back to God...the trinity is born."

11. Thomas Merton, *New Seeds of Contemplation*, p. 42.

12. Johannes Metz, *Poverty of Spirit* (Paramus, N.J.: Paulist Press, 1968), trans. by John Drury.

13. Johannes Metz, *Poverty of Spirit*.

14. John Dunne, *The Reasons of the Heart*, p. 47.

15. Johannes Metz, *Poverty of Spirit*, p. 33.

16. John Dunne, *The House of Wisdom* (New York: Harper & Row, 1985), p. 159.

17. John Dunne, *The House of Wisdom*, esp. Chapter 5, "The Heart Speaks," pp. 94-115.

18. Jane Bannard Greene and M.D. Herter Norton, *Letters of Rainer Maria Rilke: 1892-1910* (New York: W.W. Norton & Co., 1969), pp. 57-58. (Letter to Emanuel von Bodman, Aug. 17, 1904).

19. *Letters of Rainer Maria Rilke*, p. 58.

Chapter 3—Obedience to an Interior Vocation

Opening Quotes: May Sarton, *Journal of a Solitude* (New York: W.W. Norton & Co., 1973), p. 57. Adrian van Kaam, *Spirituality and the Gentle Life* (Denville, N.J.: Dimension Books, 1974), p. 179.

1. May Sarton, *Journal of a Solitude*, pp. 102-103.

2. May Sarton, *Journal of a Solitude*, p. 103.

3. A similar passage of the effect of love is found in José Ortega Y Gasset, *On Love: Aspects of a Single Theme*, pp. 15-16. It is an appropriate description of the way Hannah and Will's life touched people.

4. Charles Maes, "Silence and Divine Encounter," *Envoy*, Feb. 1980, Vol. XVII, No. 20.

5. Simone Weil, *Waiting for God* (New York: Harper & Row, 1973), trans. by Emma Crawford, pp. 43-58.

6. Martin Buber, *The Legend of the Baal-Shem* (New York: Schocken Books, 1969), trans. by Maurice Friedman. See pp. 17-32, 214, 220-221.

7. Martin Buber, *The Legend of the Baal-Shem*, pp. 23-32.

8. Adrian van Kaam, *Spirituality and the Gentle Life*, p. 176.

9. Hugo Rahner, *Man at Play* (New York: Herder and Herder, 1972), p. 65.

10. Edith Hamilton, *Mythology*, pp. 87-88.

11. Adrian van Kaam, *Spirituality and the Gentle Life*, p. 178.

12. Adrian van Kaam, *Spirituality and the Gentle Life*, p. 179.

13. Joseph Kockelmans, *Martin Heidegger: A First Introduction to His Philosophy* (Pittsburgh: Duquesne Univ. Press, 1965), pp. 78-81.

14. Joseph Kockelmans, *Martin Heidegger*, pp. 78-81.

15. John Macquarrie, *An Existentialist Theology* (London: SCM Press, 1960), pp. 100-101.

16. Genesis 4:9.

17. St. John of the Cross, *Collected Works*, pp. 154-155.

18. St. John of the Cross, *Collected Works*, pp. 154-155.

19. Simone Weil, *Waiting for God*. See "Hesitations Concerning Baptism," pp. 43-57, esp. p. 48.

20. St. John of the Cross, *Collected Works*, p. 154-155. Simone Weil, *Waiting for God*.

21. Thomas Merton, *New Seeds of Contemplation*, p. 42. See also *Ascent to Truth*.

22. Simone Weil, *Waiting for God*.

23. Adrian van Kaam, *Formation of the Human Heart*, vol. III, p. 108. See also his *Envy and Originality* (Garden City, N.Y.: Doubleday, 1972).

24. Thomas Merton, *New Seeds of Contemplation*, p. 42.

25. Jane Bannard Greene and M.D. Herter Norton, *Letters of Rainer Maria Rilke*.

26. Adrian van Kaam, *Formation of the Human Heart*, pp. 66, 129, 186, 227, 307, 309.

Chapter 4—A Passion for Reform

Opening Quote: Adrian van Kaam, *Spirituality and the Gentle Life* (Denville, N.J.: Dimension Books, 1974), p. 85.

1. Adrian van Kaam, *Formation of the Human Heart*. John Macquarrie, *An Existentialist Theology*, pp. 110-111. Bernard Boelen, *Personal Maturity: The Existential Dimension* (New York: Seabury Press, 1978). See esp. Chapters 2, 3, 7, 8.

2. John Macquarrie, *An Existentialist Theology*.

3. Adrian van Kaam, *Formation of the Human Heart*, p. 165.

4. Carol Tavris, *Anger, the Misunderstood Emotion* (New York: Simon & Schuster, 1982). Leslie Allen Paul, author of *Angry Young Man* (London: Faber and Faber, 1951), and John Osborne, author of the play *Look Back in Anger* (New York: Criterion Books, 1957), have become synonymous with anger as a creative vehicle for the expression of authenticity.

5. José Ortega Y Gasset, *On Love: Aspects of a Single Theme*, Chapter 1.

6. See Carol Tavris, *Anger, the Misunderstood Emotion*; William Kraft, *A Psychology of Nothingness* (Philadelphia: Westminster, 1974), pp. 55-58. Paul S. Fiddes, *The Creative Suffering of God* (Oxford: Clarendon, 1992).

7. José Ortega Y Gasset, *On Love: Aspects of a Single Theme*. He indicates "taking notice" in the first moment of the experience of love.

8. Martin Heidegger, *Being and Time* (New York: Harper & Row, 1962), trans. by John Macquarrie and Edward Robinson, pp. 237-238.

9. George Orwell, *Nineteen Eighty-Four* (New York: Signet, New American Library, 1949). Upton Sinclair (1878-1968), author of more than eighty books, is noted for his social and political sensitivity. His book *Jungle* reputedly influenced President Theodore Roosevelt and resulted in the 1906 Food and Drug Act.

10. Robert Bolt, *A Man for All Seasons* (New York: Vintage Books, 1962).

Chapter 5—The Ascetics of Intimacy

Opening Quotes: St. John of the Cross, *Collected Works* (Washington, D.C.: I.C.S. Publications, 1991), p. 118, trans. by Kieran Kavanaugh and Otilio Rodriguez. George MacDonald, *Sir Gibbie* (Philadelphia: J.B. Lippincott & Co., 1879), p. 75.

1. F. Scott Fitzgerald, *The Crack-Up* (New York: New Directions, 1956), p. 69.

2. F. Scott Fitzgerald, *The Crack-Up*, p. 69.

3. F. Scott Fitzgerald, *The Crack-Up*, p. 69.

4. F. Scott Fitzgerald, *The Crack-Up*, p. 70.

5. St. Teresa of Avila, *The Collected Works of St. Teresa of Avila* (Washington, D.C.: I.C.S. Publications, 1987), trans. by Kieran Kavanaugh and Otilio Rodriguez. See vol. I, pp. 164, 165, 242, 257, 270, 336, 355-357, 384; vol. II, pp. 293, 294, 310, 420-421.

6. Adrian van Kaam, *Formation of the Human Heart*. For a further elaboration on the role of humor in promoting detachment, see also pp. 25-30.

7. Adrian van Kaam, *Formation of the Human Heart*, p. *xix*.

8. Samuel Beckett, *Waiting for Godot* (New York: Grove Press, 1954).

9. John Dunne, *Reasons of the Heart*, p. 48.

10. Hugo Rahner, *Man at Play*, pp. 26-45.

11. Hugo Rahner, *Man at Play*, pp. 26-45.

12. St. John of the Cross, *Collected Works*, esp. pp. 155, 375-376.

13. Dorothee Soëlle, *Suffering* (Philadelphia: Fortress Press, 1984), pp. 13-16.

14. *The Compact Edition of the Oxford English Dictionary* (Oxford, England: Oxford Univ. Press, 1979), p. 291.

15. St. John of the Cross, *Collected Works*, pp. 353-457.

16. Sr. Rose Clarisse Gadoury, "Loneliness and Intimacy," unpublished lecture, Anna Maria College, Paxton, Mass., Oct. 1976.

17. See footnote 5.

18. Adrian van Kaam, *Formation of the Human Heart*, p. 25.

Chapter 6—Intimate Circles

Opening Quotes: George MacDonald, *Creation in Christ* (Wheaton, Ill.: Harold Shaw Publications, 1976), pp. 199-200, ed. by Rolland Hein (originally published as three volumes entitled: *Unspoken Sermons*), published in 1870, 1885, 1891, respectively; this quote appeared in Volume II, "The Creation of Sons," sermon 18, subtitled "Life." Robert Herrick, *Poems of Love* (New York: Avenel Books, 1989), ed. by Gail Harvey, p. 64.

1. Adrian van Kaam, *Formation of the Human Heart*, p. 216.

2. Thomas Tyrrell, "Intimacy, Asceticism and Infatuation," in *Studies in Formative Spirituality: Spirituality and Sexuality* (Pittsburgh: Duquesne Univ. Press, Feb. 1981, Vol. II, No. 1.), pp. 99-110. (The description incorporates minor revision and is based upon protocol data.)

3. Thomas Tyrrell, "From Courtship to Intimacy: The Marital Journey," in *Studies in Formative Spirituality: Marriage and Spiritual Formation.* (Pittsburgh: Duquesne Univ. Press, May 1985, Vol. VI, No. 2), pp. 255-269.

4. Martin Heidegger, *Being and Time*.

5. Thomas Merton, *New Seeds of Contemplation*, p. 42; see also Chapter 21. For a comprehensive presentation of Merton's construct of "true" and "false" self, see James Finley, *Merton's Palace of Nowhere* (Notre Dame, Ind.: Ave Maria Press, 1978).

6. Simone Weil, *Waiting for God*.

7. See footnote 5.

8. Adrian van Kaam, *Formation of the Human Heart*, p. 216.

9. John Dunne, *The House of Wisdom*, p. 10.

10. John Dunne, *Reasons of the Heart*, p. 58.

11. Thomas Merton, *The Wisdom of the Desert* (New York: New Directions, 1970), pp. 62-63.

12. *The Jerusalem Bible* (Garden City, N.Y.: Doubleday, 1968), p. 802.

13. *The Jerusalem Bible*, p. 1069.

14. Karl Rahner, *Theological Investigations: Further Theology of the Spiritual Life 2* (New York: Herder and Herder, 1971), trans. by David Bourke, pp. 33-50, "Ideas for a Theology of Childhood." See esp. p. 48. See also Karl Rahner and Herbert Vorgrimler, *Theological Dictionary* (New York: Herder and Herder, 1965), p. 73, where he defines "childlikeness."

15. Richard Foster, *Freedom of Simplicity* (New York: Harper & Row, 1981), p. 15.

16. Simone Weil, *Gravity and Grace* (New York: Ark Paperbacks, 1987), p. 160. Italics added.

17. Richard Foster, *Freedom of Simplicity*.

18. Stephen W. Hawking, *A Brief History of Time: From the Big Bang to Black Holes* (New York: Bantam Books, 1988).

19. Evelyn Eaton Whitehead and James D. Whitehead, *A Sense of Sexuality: Christian Love and Intimacy* (Garden City, N.Y.: Doubleday, 1989), pp. 18-89, 93, 195, 207-208, 286-292. The authors present a compelling argument for the notion of care as an *essential* feature of the formations of meaning, integrity, and depth. See also Joan Timmerman, *Sexuality and Spiritual Growth* (New York: Crossroad, 1992).

Selected Bibliography

Alberoni, Francesco. *Falling in Love*. New York: Random House, 1983, trans. Lawrence Venuti.

Dunne, John. *The Reasons of the Heart: A Journey into Solitude & Back Again into the Human Circle*. New York: Macmillan, 1978.

Fiddes, Paul. *The Creative Suffering of God*. Oxford: Clarendon Press, 1992.

Foster, Richard. *Prayer: Finding the Heart's True Home*. San Francisco: Harper & Row, 1992.

Gaylin, Willard, and Ethel Person, eds. *Passionate Attachments: Thinking About Love*. New York: The Free Press, 1988.

Gratton, Carolyn. *The Art of Spiritual Guidance*. New York: Crossroad, 1992.

Groeschel, Benedict. *Spiritual Passages*. New York: Crossroad, 1986.

Halpern, Sue. *Migrations to Solitude*. New York: Pantheon Books, 1992.

Levinson, Daniel. *The Seasons of a Man's Life*. New York: Ballantine, 1979.

Lerner, Harriet Goldhor. *The Dance of Intimacy: A Woman's Guide to Courageous Acts of Change in Key Relationships*. New York: Harper & Row, 1989.

Merton, Thomas. *New Seeds of Contemplation*. Gethsemani, Ky.: New Directions, 1961.

Miller, Jerome. *The Way of Suffering: A Geography of Crisis*. Washington, D.C.: Georgetown University Press, 1988.

Moustakas, Clark. *Loneliness and Love*. New York: Prentice Hall, 1990.

Muto, Susan. *John of the Cross for Today: The Ascent*. Notre Dame, Ind.: Ave Maria Press, 1991.

Ortega Y Gasset, José. *On Love: Aspects of a Single Theme*. New York: Meridian Books, World Publishing Co., 1966.

Soëlle, Dorothee. *Suffering*. Philadelphia: Fortress Press, 1984.

Storr, Anthony. *Solitude: A Return to the Self*. New York: The Free Press, 1988.

Tavris, Carol. *Anger: The Misunderstood Emotion*. New York: Simon & Schuster, 1982.

Timmerman, Joan. *Sexuality and Spiritual Growth*. New York: Crossroad, 1992.

Tyrrell, Thomas J. *Urgent Longings: Reflections on Infatuation, Intimacy, and Sublime Love*. Mystic, Conn.: Twenty-Third Publications, 1994, rev. ed.

Ullmann, Liv. *Changing*. New York: Bantam Books, 1978.

_____. *Choices*. New York: Alfred A. Knopf, 1984.

van Kaam, Adrian. *Formative Spirituality: The Formation of the Human Heart*. New York: Crossroad, 1986.

_____. *Spirituality and the Gentle Life*. Denville, N.J.: Dimension Books, 1974.

Viorst, Judith. *Necessary Losses*. New York: Fawcett Gold Medal, 1993.

Welch, John. *When Gods Die: An Introduction to St. John of the Cross*. Mahwah, N.J.: Paulist Press, 1990.

Weldwood, John. *Journey of the Heart: Intimate Relationship and the Path of Love*. New York: HarperCollins, 1990.

Whitehead, Evelyn, and James Whitehead. *A Sense of Sexuality: Christian Love and Intimacy*. Garden City, N.Y.: Doubleday, 1989.

Of Related Interest...

Urgent Longings
Reflections on Infatuation, Intimacy, and Sublime Love
Thomas J. Tyrrell
In this study of the way human love develops into mature relationships,
the author looks at infatuation, encouraging it as a necessary step to full
intimacy with another.

ISBN: 0-89622-573-9, 128 pp, $7.95

Intimacy and the Hungers of the Heart
Pat Collins, C.M.
This work encompasses intimacy with oneself and with the created
world. The book is intended to renew dispirited Christians by providing
them with a reliable spiritual map.

ISBN: 0-89622-497-X, 240 pp, $9.95

Who We Are Is How We Pray
Matching Personality and Spirituality
Charles Keating
Draws on the 16 personality types identified in the Myers-Briggs
personality profile and matches each to a suitable form and style of
spirituality.

ISBN: 0-89622-321-3, 168 pp, $7.95

An Enneagram Guide
A Spirituality of Love in Brokenness
Éilís Bergin and Eddie Fitzgerald
A concise overview of the Enneagram; its history and how it can help
people today.

ISBN: 0-89622-564-X, 128 pp, $8.95

Available at religious bookstores or from

TWENTY-THIRD PUBLICATIONS
P.O. Box 180 • Mystic, CT 06355

1-800-321-0411